Wheeling Decorating Co.

IDENTIFICATION & VALUE GUIDE

James L. Webster

- CAMBRIDGE
- CENTRAL GLASS
- DEPRESSION GLASS
- FENTON
- FOSTORIA
- HALL
- HEISEY
- HOMER LAUGHLIN
- HUTSCHENREUTHER
- IMPERIAL
- LENOX
- PADEN CITY
- RUSSEL WRIGHT
- TIFFIN
- TRENTON POTTERIES
- AND MORE

cb

Dedication

Dedicated to my parents, James E. and Verna I. Webster. With them, I began a journey of curiosity, inquiry, and research, leading, I hope, to a little better understanding.

ON THE FRONT COVER:

Background: Large blue compote plate. Left to right from the top down: Gold-on-White vase, $80.00 – 120.00 (Plate 356), Tall "Calla Lily" vase, $50.00 – 75.00 (Plate 45), Tall covered candy jar, $90.00 – 135.00 (Plate 228), Gold ball vase, $90.00 – 130.00 (Plate 60), Stemware with birds, $35.00 – 55.00 (Plate 285), Heisey cruet, $260.00 – 340.00 (Plate 328), Ball jug or pitcher, $180.00 – 250.00 (Plate 66), Green ice bucket, $105.00 – 155.00 (Plate 157), Large blue compote plate, $95.00 – 140.00 (Plate 366), Covered candy dish, $75.00 – 115.00 (Plate 174).

ON THE BACK COVER:

Left to right from the top down: Small compote, $110.00 – 155.00 (Plate 341), Soup bowl and plate, $25.00 – 40.00 (Plate 301), Stemware with rooster, $40.00 – 60.00 (Plate 465), Individual teapot, $45.00 – 75.00 (Plate 95), Charger with flowered center, $110.00 – 160.00 (Plate 220), Black vase with gold design, $125.00 – 175.00 (Plate 54), Handled gold serving platter, $95.00 – 140.00 (Plate 201), Candlestick, $65.00 – 95.00 for pair (Plate 331), Vase with pheasant, $65.00 – 90.00 (Plate 259).

Cover design by Beth Summers
Book design by Karen Smith and Kelly Dowdy

COLLECTOR BOOKS
P.O. Box 3009
Paducah, Kentucky 42002-3009

www.collectorbooks.com

Copyright © 2003 James L. Webster

The current values in this book should be used only as a guide. They are not intended to set prices, which vary from one section of the country to another. Auction prices as well as dealer prices vary greatly and are affected by condition as well as demand. Neither the author nor the publisher assumes responsibility for any losses that might be incurred as a result of consulting this guide.

Searching For A Publisher?

We are always looking for people knowledgeable within their fields. If you feel that there is a real need for a book on your collectible subject and have a large comprehensive collection, contact Collector Books.

Contents

Acknowledgments

I begin this acknowledgment by saying, "We are truly thankful for the opportunity to present this information about the Wheeling Decorating Co., Inc. (WDCO) to the general public." I use "we" because it is really the people listed below, and their families, who helped make this book possible. I accept any problems, errors, misinterpretations, or misrepresentations that occur within this book as my own shortcomings. If information is correct and helpful, thank the people below. If the information is wrong or inappropriate, blame me.

Certainly, thanks are given to those individuals who provided information, photographs, literature, stories, and general information about WDCO. The interviews we held were really at the heart of the understanding we have today about the workings of WDCO. I'm sure there are many more people out there who we need to talk to about WDCO, and hopefully we will be able to find some of them. Certainly, heading the list of our interviewees, was Albert Knoblich, son of the production foreman and chief designer for Wheeling Decorating. Most of the specific historical information in this book was provided by Albert or was confirmed by him. It is Albert who has led the way over the last several years in keeping the spirit of WDCO alive. I hope that this book is at least a partial fulfillment of that spirit. Besides Albert, the other person whose vision we sought was Douglas Norman, grandson of the President of Wheeling Decorating from 1948 until 1957. Doug is an avid collector of Wheeling Decorating items and was a valuable member of our Wheeling search team. Doug made available much of his collection for photographing for this book. The counsel, encouragement, and suggestions of both Doug and Albert are greatly appreciated.

One of our earliest interviews was with Ms. Olive Muegge. Olive (92 years old in 2002) started work for WDCO at age 16 and worked in the Pattern Department from 1925 until 1942. Her thoughts about the operations at WDCO were insightful, and she also added additional information about the social atmosphere among the employees.

The family members of the leadership of WDCO were most helpful and encouraging in developing information on Wheeling Decorating. Mary Etta Norman and her sister Virginia Nolan both shared recollections of their father's (Lee Taylor) work at WDCO. Max Knoblich's son, John, also shared memories of his father's work in the acid etching room at Wheeling. Beverly Calangelo, oldest daughter of Oliver Crumley, provided a list of people she remembered working at Wheeling Decorating. Irene Crumley Dodd helped with the list of WDCO employees and shared her experiences in trying to keep WDCO an active company.

We are also grateful to the various people and organizations in Wheeling that gave us the time, support, and the use of facilities to help in our research. The Wheeling Library provided us the files of information they had on the Wheeling Decorating Company and assisted us in our research on the various individuals from the Company. They also provided us with a meeting room to allow former employees, relatives, and people with a general interest in WDCO to come together and share information. Some of the people at this meeting included: Janice Crumley George, Irene Crumley Dodd, Sylvia Milonovich, Mary Etta Norman, Nancy Tofaute, Virginia Taylor Nolan, Becky Crummett, Michael Crummett, Martha Bachman, Albert Knoblich, Helen Dunzath, Robert L. Martin, Doty Carl, and Mildred Mazelon.

As we worked our way through the research for this book, talking with a variety of specialists in the area of glassware and china revealed how little we knew about WDCO and the overall area of collecting such items. Helen Jones of "Backward Glances" was very generous in her sharing of historical trade journal information about Wheeling Decorating. We made several trips to the Fenton Glass Museum in Williamstown, West Virginia, and to the Heisey Museum in Newark, Ohio, and obtained valuable information at both places. Importantly, we want to acknowledge support from the Oglebay Institute Museum in Wheeling. This museum houses a large glass and china collection including a very nice set of decorated items from WDCO. The museum is also home to the design book that was prepared and used by Karl Knoblich. The late John Artzberger, curator, was always encouraging in his efforts to get us the information necessary to make this publication a success. Holly McCluskey, Director of Museums at Oglebay Park, has been equally encouraging to us.

Appreciation must also be given to the staff of Collector Books of Paducah, Kentucky, for being willing to undertake a project with the input coming from a group of neophytes trying to resurrect information on a company that closed 40 years ago. Their design and editorial support are greatly appreciated.

Normally, I would hesitate to include an acknowledgement to an inanimate object. Still, there can be little question about the benefit derived from the use of the Internet, particularly www.eBay.com. The inability to view and use eBay to find various examples of items decorated by WDCO would have made the development of this book a much more drawn-out process.

Many of the photographs in this book were taken by Randy Ferrell of Parkersburg, West Virginia. Again, when the photographs look good, Randy probably took them. If they are a little deficient, they were most likely taken by me.

Finally, I wish to thank my wife Marsha, my three children — Frank, Rob, and Laura — and my step-family as a whole, for giving me the encouragement, patience, and time to make this book happen. Marsha, in particular, used her years of training as a legal and judicial secretary to make sure that what was said was correct and faithful to the people from whom we obtained the information.

For well over a century the mid-Ohio Valley has been North America's leading pottery, china, and glassware production center. Areas along the Ohio River in West Virginia, Pennsylvania, and Ohio have been home to hundreds of glass manufacturers for more than 100 years. The high point of glassmaking in this region was particularly strong from the late 1880s through the 1960s. After that time there was a steady decline in numbers of producers, yet to this day several of the more prolific producers still survive. There has been much published over the years concerning the glass industry and the various glass-producing companies. Most of these publications have dealt with identification of origin and scope of production, and have been tailored to the glass collecting fraternity. The one area associated with glass manufacturing that has been overlooked until now is glass decoration.

Not all glass producers decorated their own wares, and not all glass decorators made their own glass. In many instances independent glass decorating companies existed solely to provide this valuable service. In most cases these decorating companies were much smaller than the producers and very little artifactual material was ever saved or documented. This obscurity and omission has left a tremendous void in the world of glass research. Many collectors and researchers of American glass often run into dead-ends when trying to identify the makers and decorators of individual pieces of glass. Sadly, there has been a lack of source information to consult to help answer their queries.

Now, Mr. Webster has presented the research and collector communities with a very valuable tool. His research into one of the most prolific of the Mid-Ohio Valley decorating companies, the Wheeling Decorating Company, will prove to be of great significance in the forwarding of glass research and identification for the advanced researcher and the novice collector alike. Jim's research into the activities and production of this instrumental decorating company comes at a critical time. He has managed to gather first-hand accounts and recollections from individuals that were directly involved with and worked at the company. This first-hand accountability is priceless and provides insight that would otherwise be lost to posterity in the near future. Comprehensive documentation on glass decoration is every bit as important to researchers as the origin of manufacture. These two areas of glass production complement each other and help us reach a better understanding of the contractual world of glassmaking. The book you now hold in your hands is a giant step forward in providing comprehensive documentation and better understanding of the glass decorating world. As a member of the board of directors of a museum dedicated to the promotion of our national glassmaking heritage, I can unequivocally state that Jim's efforts will reap rewards for years to come.

Roy Ash
Board of Directors
West Virginia Museum of American Glass

This book is the direct result of the rapid information exchange afforded by the recent development of online Internet auctions. Many of these auctions deal primarily with antiques. How does one go about compiling information on a particular manufacturer of a product such as glassware or china? To find this information, it would probably take several years of searching antiques stores and traveling to many auctions. This large "time-to-find" approach is particularly true for items from moderately-sized firms or for items which were of limited distribution. The Internet has provided a ready and rapid source for viewing and, at least partly, understanding what might be available about or from a given manufacturer. There are other ways to gain information on a given type of item or a particular manufacturing firm; either find an expert on the topic who has a large collection, or find significant information in published literature. Sadly, neither of these was readily available when we started trying to find details on the Wheeling Decorating Company (WDCO).

Why our interest in WDCO? For 30 years I have primarily been a collector of primitive Americana and antique tools. Why the change? My wife, Marsha, was looking for some pieces of WDCO to give as a gift to a son-in-law. It turns out that his grandfather lived in Wheeling, West Virginia, and was the president of WDCO from 1948 to 1957. I asked Marsha what she knew about WDCO. She said very little information was available, as far as she knew. My research quickly verified this and started us on the path of determining what really took place at WDCO. It was the Internet (mostly eBay.com) that gave us insight into the variety of items manufactured by WDCO, along with a small amount of additional data, such as logos and supply sources. I am not a stranger to research, having spent most of my career (Ph.D., chemical engineering) doing just that for a large chemical corporation. I am not an expert on china, porcelain, or glass, nor will I ever be. That truly requires a "wide-field" expert to deal with such a category. The work presented here is more of a singular guide, not only to the specialists, but also to casual readers trying to gain information on the WDCO products and their values. As you go through this book, you will see that much of the evolutionary information is sketchy, at best. This is where both the specialist and the casual collector can be of great assistance. Any information that can be provided about WDCO, its products, or its suppliers, is important for expanding the current database. Even small pieces of information such as "where" or "when" about a given WDCO item can be helpful. Knowing more about what firm produced one of the china, pottery, or glass blanks decorated by WDCO is also useful. Any information that can be shared will be greatly appreciated. Helpful input may be sent to the address below. I've also included an e-mail address which may be a better starting point to contact me. If I can gather enough new information, I will consider issuing a second edition of this book.

James L. Webster
202 North Hills Drive
Parkersburg, WV 26104-9232
wdco@charter.net

Notes and Conventions

The current values in this book should be used as guides only. They are not intended to set prices. The market itself will do that, particularly when items are being sold on the Internet. Certainly, regional differences will come into play, as will availability and condition. Neither the author nor the publisher assumes any responsibility for any losses or gains that might be incurred as a result of consulting this guide.

The author, in writing this book, is aware of the impact that first-time awareness has with any product. The awareness in this case stems from the fact that, other than for trademarked items, most collectors were unaware that the items they purchased were decorated by the Wheeling Decorating Company. Does this awareness increase the value of an item? It probably will. But put another way, we are very certain, because of the overall quality of this company, that knowing it is Wheeling Decorating will not decrease an item's value. With that said, we will try to explain the factors we used in reaching the value ranges shown in this book.

We know that regional factors are true and do affect selling price, particularly in an antique store or antique mall. This is part of the reason we have shown a range of pricing in this book. Still, the Internet has become somewhat of a leveling factor. What is put online in New York City may well be sold in New Orleans or in Stillwater, Oklahoma. The Internet has many problems, though. The problem when you can't hold an item in your hand is the characterization of the item you are considering buying. What does it mean when the seller says, "It is really of top quality and a very nice addition for your collection?" Define "top quality" and "very nice." What are these terms? One must have better qualitative terms than these. It is a lot like the word "vintage." For some individuals it means contemporary, while for others it means very old. It is much better to use a date with "vintage," of 1920 vintage, for example. The meaning of words given by one person is not the same to another person. In addition, poor to fair quality pictures on the Internet can be very deceiving. Some people feel that the design patterns are unimportant, and don't give a photographic close-up of the decorating. Or, they say it is in perfect condition, with 95 percent of its gold still intact. That's like saying a car is in perfect condition, with 95 percent of the paint intact. This is not a tirade. This is to tell you that in the great majority of cases you can control the outcome. Use your e-mail, ask the tough questions, get better pictures, and above all, get assurances as to the quality. If someone won't deal with you on that basis, it's time to look elsewhere. You are the one who decides what you are willing to pay for a given quality. But you should ask the seller and get as much information as possible. It takes time, but that's part of building a good collection.

When dealing with quality, we have used a six-level evaluation process. See the quality scale table below.

Pristine means that an item has most likely never been used and is free from any manufactured defects such as air bubbles, straws, small bumps, etc., and free from all decorating defects. Excellent requires much the same standard but the item may have seen some small and gentle use. Still, there should be no damage, chip repairs, manufactured defects or decorating defects.

A Very good rating may show some slight manufactured blemishes such as small air bubbles and pinpoint bumps – and maybe even a little rub in the decoration. But these generally can be found only with careful screen-

Quality Scale	
Level	*Value*
Poor	10
Fair	20
Good	40
Very good	80
Excellent	100
Pristine	120 – 300

ing. Professionally repaired items, of otherwise excellent condition, often fall into this category, too. The next level, good, is the first level where the faults are readily assessable by touch and looks. For most serious collectors, this is the lowest level of acceptability. These collectors are usually looking for a way to trade up to the next level when they have these items. With a good rating, decorating designs are still totally visible, though there may be the slightest of thinning of enamels and gold. Thus, a well worn vase or evenly worn salt shaker would not qualify for the good level. The wear of these items often occurs in a raised area of an etched or enameled pattern. Unless it is a real rarity, items in the good category have not been professionally repaired to raise them to that level. But these items do often see amateur repairs.

The fair level (or lower) is the place we relegate items when the seller says, "There is still 95 percent of the gold or enamel left." Minute chips and dings, color fading, and blemishes are to be expected. There are lots of non-professional repairs made in this category but by doing them, the items may pass as a non-critical display piece. The poor level is just that — poor and you don't want it. Still, it can be used to collect information about a pattern or design. And, if it is a rarity, it may just be a starting point for an upgrading process. But it is never for display.

We've included a grading scale along with the named level scale for quality. In its format and form, it is very simple. If you are offered an item of an agreed-to level of good, you would expect to pay about 40 percent of what you would pay for an excellent graded item. Thus, quality has a real premium. Or, if the item was very good you could expect to pay 80 percent of the excellent value. Pristine items can cost several times what an excellent item might cost.

On top of the quality factor for pricing, there is also the availability question. Here also, we have developed a unique six-level scale. For our work with the Wheeling Decorating items, we have assigned a rough but very useable availability factor; how often does the item show up on the Internet. The availability table below will show our experience factors.

This availability scale works for Wheeling items but would be significantly different for another line of collectibles. Still, any collector can make up their own table for their line of interest just by using the practical experience from the Internet. What one

finds is that this information translates well to shopping in antique malls and stores. But beware, for if some pattern or item does not have an inherent appeal unto itself, availability may mean little.

In Chapter 5, we provide descriptions of the various items we have chosen. In this section we first show a photograph or plate number so we can make reference to the item. Then, we name the item in a general way, e.g., creamer and sugar bowl. Next, we give the size of the item, or if there is more than one item, we give sizes, going left to right. Thus, the creamer might be 3.4h x 4d, and the sugar bowl 4.1h x 6.2l x 4.2w. All dimensions are in inches unless otherwise specified. The table below shows the various abbreviations used.

At times an item may not be round but a diameter value is still given as an easy approximation of its size. Thus, an eight-sided tray may have a diameter given.

Next, a design number and a design name are shown. These are listed in Chapter 6 for the different

Abbreviations
h	Height — at the highest point
l	Length — at the point of greatest length
w	Width — at the widest point
d	Diameter — at the point of the largest diameter
sq	Square item

Wheeling patterns. D-7 is a design pattern and its name is listed as "Roses and Thorns." Next comes a trademark identification (usually on china and pottery items) and it might be listed as TM-H, which was a fairly large, etched, diamond-shaped, gold-encrusted logo. Wheeling often had numbers on the bottom of its china to show which company had produced the blank that was to be decorated (see Chapter 7). If there were a blank number it would be shown handwritten e.g., 630. Then, if the company associated with this number were known, it would be given, e.g., Hall China Company. Often, only a company name or perhaps just a country of origin would be available and these would be listed in the same manner. This information is followed by pricing information. The values given are a range for items of very good to excellent quality. This value varies with not only the quality range, but the availability, pricing history, location, and season of the year. Generally there is a lower value during the summer months. A cream and sugar set that usually sells for about $45.00 – 55.00 may only bring $35.00 – 45.00 during the summer. Antique stores and malls will invariably have summer sales to try and keep their sales volume up.

Additional reference information may also be added, such as the fact that the pattern may be similar to pattern D-23, and so forth. Other notes could contain the information that the item had a sticker from a store in Cincinnati. Thus, information which

Availability
Level	Frequency
Abundant	Can always be found online
Plentiful	Usually can be found
Reasonable	Comes up every couple of weeks
Infrequent	Seen once a month
Scarce	Seen a couple of times a year
Rare	Can find once a year or less

we might include under a photograph of a cup and saucer could read: Plate 999, creamer and sugar bowl, 3.4h x 4d, 4.1h x 6.2l x 4.2w, D-7, "Roses and Thorns," TM-H, blank: 630, Hall China Company, $35.00 –

55.00 per set. Note: Pattern similar to D-23. Item was originally sold in Cincinnati, Ohio.

Chapter 1: *Introduction*

Humankind has always searched for ways to express beauty in new and different ways. Many times, a utilitarian item or an item of true grace can be further enhanced by the addition of an uplifting design or pattern. This design or pattern may add beauty by its simplicity or by the greatness of its detail. For china, pottery, porcelain, and glassware, this was a role often carried out by decorating companies during the first half of the twentieth century. The Wheeling Decorating Company was one of the outstanding companies that produced such work.

A disturbing thing for a collector of manufactured items is not to know who made the item or who decorated it. When collecting glassware, china, and pottery, a brand name is important not only to give a sense of value, but a sense of the history that goes along with the item. Certainly a sense of ambience and beauty are important to the item, but knowing if that item were produced or decorated by a particular manufacturer adds connectivity to the entire history of its existence. Names like Heisey, Tiffin, Cambridge, Limoges, Fenton, Homer Laughlin, Hall, Hutschenreuther, Steubenville, and many others, add to the feeling of understanding that gives this collecting its connectivity. Yet, for more than 50 years, collectors often had decorated items with which they could not make the final connection. Who provided that value-adding enamel or gold decoration? Where did a given design pattern come from? One of the larger U. S. decorating firms for glass, china, and pottery was the Wheeling Decorating Company (usually referred to as WDCO or just Wheeling) of Wheeling, West Virginia. It decorated items (purchased blanks) probably from more than 300 companies around the world. While many of the china and pottery items were marked with the Wheeling logo, the design patterns used on these items probably numbered less than 50. Since almost none of the glassware was marked with the Wheeling logo, owners of decorated glass did not know if their particular item was decorated with one of the more than 600 patterns used by WDCO or by some other company. Quality decorations always add value to glassware. Glassware collectors will be especially pleased to see for the first time the wide range of designs used by WDCO. Invariably, they are the work of a team of skilled crafts people. People who are collectors of glassware from America's glass belt, along and close to the Ohio River, will find this WDCO book to be of particular help in identifying etched gold and enameled items they might have in their collections.

When preparing a book of this type, one can usually look at four aspects for the division of information. Most important to the purchaser is the photographic and pricing information presented with the various items of the collecting area. Second, the history and understanding of the activities of the producing company is enlightened by the understanding of the economic and political issues of the time. Third, and what is often a driving point for the author, is the search for items made by the producing company, how they were made, when they were made, and the many interactions this search provides. Finally, the fourth part of the book would include all the other items such as a preface, acknowledgments, notes and conventions, references, etc. Then, taken as a whole, one can have a definitive work about a company, or at least a jumping-off point for the further collection and dissemination of information about the company. This study of the Wheeling Decorating Company is a starting point for not only sharing but hopefully for collecting more information. Less than one-third of the available patterns and designs of this company have been found as of 2002. Yet, since the patterns were put on other companies' products, both generalized and specific collectors will surely find many more examples of the artwork of WDCO within the next few years. This will allow interested parties to participate in this renewed search for historical verification of the products of WDCO. Additional information will also surface about the history of WDCO and the people who worked there. All of this adds to the mystique of the Wheeling Decorating Company and gives interested collectors an opportunity to add to the understanding of WDCO.

The history of the Wheeling Decorating Company (WDCO) is difficult to map out as there are very few records about the company. Though WDCO was in business from 1900 until 1962, little historical information has been found. Few books contain information about WDCO. When looking for information on back-stamp logos or marks, we found only *Lehner's Encyclopedia of U. S. Marks on Pottery, Porcelain & Clay* (page 516 of reference 5 in Bibliography) showed any of the WDCO backstamps or trademarks. That book showed just two out of the 12 or so logos that WDCO used. The 12 lines of biographical data given were the most found in any reference book. As stated earlier, part of the problem with the information sources for Wheeling Decorating is the fact that they were a decorating company, not a glass or porcelain/china manufacturing company. They bought only other companies' products and added value to these items with their unique decorating skills. While Pickard China of Chicago (one of WDCO's competitors) did much the same, by 1937 Pickard had developed its own world class china manufacturing process.

The early history of WDCO is primarily that of two men: Frank Herman Thurm, owner, and Karl J. Knoblich, designer/artist. This is not to say there were not other significant individuals involved with the company. It is just that up to 1947 or so, these two men were at the heart of the decision-making process for much of what WDCO did.

Much of the information and understandings about WDCO is the result of the efforts of Albert K. Knoblich, Karl's son. Albert was in a unique position. In 1934, when he was in the fifth grade, his mother died. After her death, each morning he would go to work with his father, then go to school. After school, he would again come back to WDCO and wait for his father until it was time to go home. Thus, over the years he developed a first-hand knowledge of what was taking place in the manufacturing end of the business. Karl also had a daughter, Charlotte Dennis, who has a unique collection of WDCO items.

Albert Knoblich's efforts have gone far in helping to keep a high level of interest in Wheeling Decorating. He continues to give talks about WDCO to residents in the Wheeling area. He has also provided educational information to the glass museum at Wheeling's Oglebay Park. There is a collection of WDCO items at Oglebay Institute Glass Museum, including the pattern design book made by Karl Knoblich. It is this design book which has been so very helpful in determining which glassware items were decorated by WDCO since there are no WDCO logos used on the glassware they decorated. Much of the historical data given below comes from Albert and from the very few newspaper articles and other articles that were written on special Wheeling Decorating occasions and anniversaries.

The Beginning Years 1869 – 1911

Frank Herman Thurm was born on March 5, 1869, in Dresden, Germany. While not much is known about his early years, he did grow up in Dresden. At that time, Dresden was known as a great glass center. After an early education in Dresden, his obituary, in the local *Rotarian* magazine, stated he went to Teplitz, Bohemia, which later became part of Czechoslovakia. It was in Teplitz where he trained as an artist and took up decorating glassware and china. To further expand and improve his understanding of the decorative arts, he took a position with the famous exporting business, House of Walis, in Vienna, Austria, a decorating shop of the highest quality. In 1893, at the age of 24, the lure of the New World attracted him, and he left Vienna and came to the United States, settling in Wheeling, West Virginia.

The choice of Wheeling would seem fairly natural for him in 1893. Probably the largest concentration of glass, porcelain, and pottery firms in the United States were then located within 100 miles of Wheeling. More than 20 glassware firms were within 60 miles, mostly along a Pittsburgh-Wheeling corridor and directly west into Ohio. It is little wonder that this Ohio, Pennsylvania, and West Virginia area is often called the "Glass Belt" (Bibliography, reference 1, page 796). While much can be said about the glass business in this area, the pottery, porcelain, and china business was just as strong or stronger. From Zanesville, Ohio (Weller Pottery, Roseville Pottery) to Wheeling, West Virginia (Wheeling Pottery, Warwick China), north to Steubenville, Ohio (Steubenville Pottery) and East Liverpool, Ohio, (Sebring Pottery, Homer Laughlin China, Harker Pottery, Hall China, Knowles, Taylor & Knowles), these businesses were plentiful. East Liverpool, alone had more than 20 such firms at that time. Without doubt, the Ohio River played an important role in all of these commercial ventures. Most appropriately, this area in this time period could be called the Great Glass and Porcelain Beltway.

It is unclear where Frank Thurm first found employment in the Wheeling area. Reportedly, it was with a firm called the Ohio Valley China Company which went out of the decorating business sometime after 1893. Still, many have said that in any industry, even in the glass and china companies of the early 1900s, shut-

Plate 2-1. Frank Thurm, 1869 – 1949. Owner of the Wheeling Decorating Company 1900 – 1949.

downs, buy-outs, and consolidations are an important part of the growth and expansion necessary to carry the industry forward. Certainly, these steps promoted the interchange of ideas, both from artistic and technological points of view. These consolidations also led to much confusion as to who did what or who made what, which has important ramifications for a company such as Wheeling Decorating. As the interchanges of ideas, designs, and techniques grew, many of the manufacturers of plain glass or china began detailed decorating themselves. Thus, a given piece of glassware, like a Tiffin wine glass, could have been decorated by a variety of different firms, including the Tiffin Company itself. There also appears to have been somewhat of a "rip-off" market where one firm's designs were modified slightly by another firm and then used by the second firm to help gain market entry. Some of these, like the copying of early European designs, were done with elegance, but many can also be considered low quality fakes. Still, with all of this going on, the early 1900s certainly were a growth period for the Great Glass and Porcelain Beltway of the Ohio River eastern drainage area.

Without much question wherever he had been employed, Frank Thurm had developed good skills as a decorator. It is interesting to note that Thurm, being a German native, felt that German craftsmanship was superior to all others. Where later on other decorating firms would look to France and other countries for their top quality china, Thurm favored German/Bavarian items. Many of the items Thurm used to decorate his home, including glass for windows, were imported from Germany. He began looking for ways to expand into a business of his own in the late 1890s. In 1900, he started a new decorating business. From the available sources it is not clear if Robert Engelhardt, another employee from the Ohio Valley China Company, joined forces with him in 1900 or if he joined Thurm in another move in 1904. Initially, the business was operated out of an old clubhouse located at the intersection of Mount Wood and National Road.

This business was at this location for four years. An article in the January 19, 1936 *Wheeling News-Register* (see Appendix A) stated that during those first four years, "Frank Thurm followed the orthodox American fashion of glass decorating which was to apply color by the mere application of a brush with some paint on the business end of it." The business must have been doing fairly well since the article continued, "In 1904 Frank Thurm had become quite substantial and really started business in a rather large way." It further stated that he and Robert Engelhardt, "took over what was the old Kenny Brewery building at Market and Seventh Streets." This was to be the home for the Wheeling Decorating Company for the next 58 years. It is unclear when the name Wheeling Decorating was first used. Albert Knoblich remembers seeing a plate in an antique shop in Columbus, Ohio, which had marked on the back, "Frank Thurm China Co., Whg. W. Va." Today, he regrets not buying it. We have no pieces with this logo.

While the 1936 *Wheeling News-Register* indicated that Frank Thurm was doing well, it may be that he and his partner had some financial support from relatives that helped them to move into the Market and Seventh street location. In 1903, Frank had married Carrie Kalbitzer, whose family owned the Kalbitzer Hardware Company. Engelhardt was related to Louis Bertschy of the Bertschy Furniture Company. The suggestion would be that these two families helped fund the expansion of the business. How the business grew and survived over the next seven years is unclear. Nor is it clear how long Robert Engelhardt was with the business. In the *Wheeling Business Registry*, Robert Engelhardt was shown as working for Wheeling Decorating from 1904 to 1906. From 1907 through 1920 he was listed as a decorator at WDCO. It could be that Frank Thurm bought out his partner in 1906 but Robert stayed on as a decorator through 1920. Interestingly, he did list himself as a glass decorator for the years 1915 and 1916. No occupation was listed for Engelhardt in 1921 and 1922 but in 1923 and 1924, his occupation was listed as a potter. Perhaps he had gone into business for himself.

While there is very little information on WDCO from 1900 to 1910, it is the next phase that really starts the business down the path that defines it as the Wheeling Decorating Company.

The Growth Years 1911 – 1947

We've called 1911 through 1947 the growth years primarily to honor Karl Knoblich. Certainly, there were ups and downs during this time period, not unlike many of the other glass manufacturing and decorating companies in the United States. Two World Wars and the Great Depression all had adverse affects on Wheeling Decorating and the china/pottery/glass industry as a whole. A very good history of the glass business during the first 60 years or so of the twentieth century is given in the booklet, *A. H. Heisey & Company – A Brief History* (See reference 2 in the Bibliography).

In 1911, the story goes that Frank Thurm took the train to New York City, searching for a production foreman. It is unclear what Robert Engelhardt's actual role was in the business at that time. It is known that Frank Thurm was not successful with his trip to New York and he caught the return train to Wheeling. It was on this return trip that Thurm ran into a young man who was on his way to Los Angeles seeking work. This young man was Karl Knoblich. At that time Karl was 25 years old. He had begun learning china decorating skills at the age of 14 while working at Meissen and Villeroy & Brock in Dresden, Germany. He was trained to be an artist, but obviously paid close attention to all that was going on around him in these production/decorating companies. After serving required time in the German Army, Karl is said to have become a motorcycle racer. After two years and having wrecked his motorcycle, Karl decided to go to Australia since he did not want to serve a "refresher course" in the German Army. His plans were thwarted when he couldn't get a boat to Australia for six weeks. So, to earn money, he took a job as a stoker on a boat going to New York. When Karl got to New York, he was so enthralled with the city that he jumped ship, even though he had no money. He borrowed 25¢ from a woman grocer and started searching for work. He found there was porcelain decorating work in the area. He spent the next few years in New York and New Jersey further utilizing his skills and gaining additional operational knowledge of the decorating business. Still, the lure of adventure called Karl and in 1911 he took a train and headed west for Los Angeles. Regardless of how it all happened, the chance meeting with Frank Thurm on that train changed the lives of both men. Frank Thurm would be freed up to concentrate on methods of expanding the business and Karl would take over the day-to-day production end of the business. There Karl would be able to use his decorating and creative skills, as well as the knowledge he had learned for the overall operations of a china/glass decorating business.

Our ability to follow the happenings of the Wheeling Decorating Company after Karl Knoblich arrived is limited. There are only three main sources, none of which are official company records: 1) Karl Knoblich's first design book, 2) a limited amount of information that was carried in national trade journals, magazines, and newspapers, and 3) information from interviews with a few remaining employees and/or their relatives.

The story of Karl's design book is very fascinating. When my wife joined me on our first trip to the Oglebay Park Museum in Wheeling, we were uncertain as to what we would find. We talked to, John Artzberger (now deceased), the Oglebay Institute Museum curator, and he had invited us to come and see what they had. There had been a few small showings of WDCO items at the museum, but most of these were of items that were borrowed from family members or individuals who had worked at WDCO. The last show of such items was in August of 1994. We found that the museum had a registry of more than 60 pieces, but the most interesting item was the last one on the list: the design manual of Karl Knoblich. Yes, we guess one could call this design manual an official company record, but we view it as more of a "creativity" record. It was really an artist's sketch-book in which Karl had made the detailed drawings of the various patterns that were to be used in the decorating processes. Sometimes, the actual transfer tracing from the etched metal or stone plate was included in the manual. We will go into the details of how these designs were transferred onto the various blanks in Chapter 5. Each of the designs was assigned a "D" number and many times this number appeared on the bottom of the decorated item, often when there was no other WDCO identification. The most common WDCO pattern is "D-11," which is frequently mistaken for a

Pickard pattern called "Rose and Daisy." The D-11 pattern is used almost exclusively on "All-Over-Gold" (AOG) items and distinctly differs from the Pickard pattern because it has a pair of doves worked into the design. The proper name for D-11 would be "Doves, Roses, and Daisies." Most people shorten it by calling it the "Doves" design.

The discovery of Karl's design book was eye-opening to us. We had been collecting WDCO china intensely

Karl Knoblich, 1886 – 1948. Foreman, designer, and artist at Wheeling Decorating Company from 1911 – 1948.

for nine months with the hope of writing a book about it. The design patterns used on china/porcelain blanks are few (about 50) and since china is opaque, the WDCO logos, in one form or another, are usually on the bottom of the item being decorated. These logos were the primary sources for knowing what was really decorated by WDCO. With Karl's design patterns, a whole new area was opened up — collecting specific design patterns on glass, without the need for any other identifying marks that showed the decorating had been done by WDCO. As it turns out, WDCO's decorating on glass was a much larger volume business than its china/porcelain work. While Heisey Glass (A. H. Heisey & Company of Newark, Ohio) appears to be the largest source of early glass "blanks" that WDCO used, many other names are also found which show designs developed by Karl Knoblich. The list also includes H. Northwood & Co. of Wheeling West Virginia, Fenton Art Glass of Williamstown, West Virginia, Tiffin Glass Co. of Tiffin, Ohio, Imperial Glass Co. of Bellaire, Ohio, Fostoria Glass Co. of Fostoria, Ohio, Cambridge Glass Co. of Cambridge, Ohio, and many others. Importantly, WDCO, and the buying public, saw merit in taking elegant varieties of glassware and, through the addition of gold and enameling, adding beauty and value. Much truth is seen in this as a number of glassware manufacturing firms developed their own decorating departments.

The discovery of Karl's design book is probably the most fortuitous event for our ability to know "what's what" as far as WDCO is concerned. Without this design book, almost all of the WDCO glass items would fall into an area of sheer speculation. The earliest patterns in the design book are represented by ink tracings taken from the etched metal plates that were used to make the designs that were placed on the china or glassware. It was not until design D-26 that Karl began making very formal colored sketches in the design book. It was from these colored drawings that he made the etched plates. A few times he included both the colored drawing and the black ink tracing from the etched metal plate. Each design in the book has a sequential "D" numbering system. We have followed this system in listing the designs in Chapter 6.

A single "D" design number was used on two of the design manual pages, but there is more than one item on a page. When that occurs, we have assigned different letters to the "D" number to indicate each different design. Design 204 is a good example of this as there are ten different patterns on that page. We assigned D-204a to the pattern closest to the written number and then tried to move clockwise around the page numbering each item. Thus, the next pattern would be D-204b, then D-204c, and so on.

Almost all of the pages in the design book are loose from their original binding. These pages were in disarray when we first viewed the book and a few of the patterns were even missing from their numbered locations. There was also a very large number of sketches, preliminary sketches, photographs, reverse photographs, and ink transfer designs that were found loosely stuck between many of the pages of the book. These will eventually be matched with their proper design locations in the book. Still, there are 200 – 300 of these loose sketches and other items which are of much interest and much value as far as understanding WDCO. There were more than 20 pages of detailed designs of churches and homes, generally to be put on porcelain dinner plates. There was also a small amount of generalized documentation (one listing on the back of a calendar page from May 10, 1927) included with these other loose design items.

While it is impossible to totally verify that the very earliest parts of the sketch-book designs were done by Karl Knoblich, examination of the handwriting associated with the designs leads to the conclusion that they were all done by Karl. There are 328 numbered designs in Karl's manual. On designs D-325 through D-328, Karl had written "new book" or "in new book." Obviously, he had filled the first volume and was going on to volume II. Sadly, we have no idea where this second volume is or even if it exists. We estimate that the first volume was completely filled by 1940.

Later in this book one will see "D" numbers that are higher than D-328. We do know of a large number of designs that are known to be WDCO that were not in Karl's design manual or were loose and unnumbered. We have assigned "D" numbers and descriptions to these items, beginning with the number D-600. That way if the other design manual is ever found, we hope to be able to avoid at least part of the confusion arising from double numbering. Thus, we are deliberately skipping more than 270 numbers that Karl may have assigned to some unknown designs. We know there are designs on the copies of the etching plates for which we have no assigned "D" numbers. There are three known different sets of birds.

12

But one set is numbered "486" on a steel etch plate, so that became the "D" number for "game birds." All of these birds are most often seen on glasses or plates. When found on china plates, they usually had one of the WDCO's logos on them. One of the classic design sets is called "Sweet Ad-Aline" and this set, which shows comic scenes of drunks, was used on barware items. The original sketch for this set is shown on page 13 and decorated items are found in Plates 446 through 451. These and the bird series were primarily hand-painted on top of black outlines transferred from the etch plates. There were also many unnumbered drawings of animals, fruit, comic dancers, and even a frog band. There are also a number of items which we have chosen not to assign a singular "D" design number. Included in this list are pictured church plates (mostly in the late 1920s to mid 1940s), pictures of individuals' homes, pictures of public buildings and public works, business logos and advertising, college and university seals, religious and fraternal organizations, and so forth. We have given them a generalized "D" design number. For example, D-600 will be assigned to all the various WDCO pictured church plates, and D-602 to school related items, and so forth. If, at some future date, it becomes desirable to expand on the listings of a generalized number, it can be easily done. As will be discussed further, many aspects of the business changed in the 40s and much of the truly "hand decorated" work was replaced with more economical "transfer work." Many of the non-specific categories listed above fall into this type of work.

Before leaving this topic, there is another grouping we have chosen not to include in the design numbering system. These are what we call "singular" items. This includes items which were usually made by employees of WDCO, but were made as gifts, usually given to family members. There were a number of talented artists working for WDCO, and there are many known examples of singular, or near singular, items made and given to wives, family members, or friends. Experimental items also fall into this group. Where shown, these items are given a D-900 number.

How did the Knoblich design book get to the Oglebay Park Museum? Sometime after WDCO had shut down, a crew of people was inside the Seventh and Market Street location clearing out the remaining items so the building could be converted into something else. Phil Maxwell, a Wheeling resident who was familiar with WDCO, was passing by and saw what was going on. He stopped and went inside to look around. He quickly spotted the old design book which was about to be thrown into a trash dumpster, and asked if he could have it. It was given to him and he, recognizing the historical value of the manual, gave it to the Oglebay Museum. It almost seems as if 90 percent of the understanding of WDCO would have been lost if Mr. Maxwell had not been timely with his interactions with the clean-up crew. Thanks for timely blessings.

Original Karl Knoblich sketch for the bar ware "Sweet Ad-Aline" series. See Plate 446 for the start of the series.

The Magic of Gold

The January, 1936 newspaper story about WDCO in the *Wheeling News-Register* told of a secret etching process that Frank Thurm had brought with him from Germany (see Appendix A). The article stated that in January of 1911, Thurm produced the first "plate-etched glass" in the United States. The article explained that as a young man he had carried the secret of the process with him from Dresden, Germany. Further, when Thurm got into the glass business at the turn of the century, plate-etching was unknown. Thurm had been doing all of his glass decorating using the traditional process of dipping a brush into the desired enamel paint. The newspaper story leaves the reader greatly confused about the process. Most etching, which was used at that time, was localized over a small area. This process was carried out by using a purchased etching paste, which contained a small amount of hydrofluoric acid. This method was expensive, hard to apply, and difficult to control. We would have to surmise from the

article (and from other knowledge of the process) that a black wax or tar pattern from an etched steel plate was transferred to a piece of glassware (or china). The glassware was then dipped into a liquid acid vat (hydrofluoric acid) where any of the glass not covered by the wax was eaten (etched) away. Thus, the portion of the glass covered by the wax was higher than the rest of the glass that had been etched and this produced a raised appearance on the pattern on the glassware. For some applications, a gold solution was applied to the item, or part of it, and the item was then heated in a furnace to bond the gold to the glass. The glassware item was then polished and made ready for sale.

It is easy to understand how a reporter might get confused as to what was etched (both the steel plate and the glass items had been etched). Even more confusing, which acids were used; hydrofluoric for glass etching, hydrochloric for metal etching, and a mixture of nitric (1 part) and hydrochloric (3 parts) for gold recovery. It is important to point out there are really two processes that the article was trying to describe. The first is the act of etching a pattern into glass or china. The second process is that of getting some type of gold solution that could be "painted" onto a product and then oven-fired so that the residual pure gold would adhere to the glass or china.

The actual operations necessary to do all of this will be covered in greater detail in Chapter 3. For now, it is enough to say that in about 1911, WDCO felt it had an etching process which was unique when compared with those of other decorating firms in the United States. Our guess is it was the hiring of Karl Knoblich that really brought to WDCO the second part of the process, the gold coating of the etched design. Frank Thurm had been in business since 1900 so if he were impressed with the plate-etching process, why had he not commercialized it before 1911? We would further surmise that Thurm knew about etching and that lots of people were trying to find better ways to get a uniform etch and get better gold adhesion to glass or china. The trick was to get pure gold into a useable solution, and it was probably Karl Knoblich who knew or learned how to do this.

The 1936 newspaper article stated that it was January of 1911 when WDCO developed the plate-etching process. Allan Reed, in his book *Collector's Encyclopedia of Pickard China*, (page 31 of reference 3 in Bibliography) points out, "One of Pickard's major achievements in 1911 was his introduction of etched china." One has to wonder if there was any direct competition between these two decorating houses. Did the plate-etching process (probably means the steel plate etching) just happen to show up at both places at about the same time? Or was it that china and glass decorating had just reached that point where etching was a necessary advancement? Certainly, if Thurm had brought the plate-etching concept with him from Germany in 1893, then the concept must have been known by others. Around the turn of the century and later, W. A. Pickard employed a number of German artists. Even if it had not been common knowledge, Pickard had enough of these decorating artists that he was sure to have heard of the concept. We tend to lean more towards the fact that plate-etching was a larger-scale process that tended to increase the creative opportunities for the decorating artists and the financial rewards for companies with which they were associated. It seems that plate-etching was one of those evolutionary processes whose time had arrived.

The development of an effective gold coating process was probably much more difficult to get right. It is known that the formulas used by Karl Knoblich were closely-guarded secrets. He did not share them with anyone. He did have a few copies of documents in old German that may give clues to the gold formulas and other formulas used in the different steps for decorating with gold. It is known that there were several formulas for bright gold and several for dull gold. Burnishing (polishing or buffing) of the gold-coated

items was necessary to bring the finish to the right level of brilliance or luster. Karl purchased gold from the U. S. government and also from the Hanovia Chemical & Mgf. Co. of East Newark, New Jersey. This latter gold came in a 100-gram bottle and was marked "Quid Bright Gold." Without much question, the Quid Bright Gold was one that had been ground to a very fine powder.

To help understand how the business was run at WDCO, it is advantageous to make comparisons with Pickard China of Chicago. Pickard China is a company that is still in operation today. Many of its early records appear to be intact. Thus, they tended to have a better sense of history than a firm like WDCO. WDCO went out of business more than 40 years ago and even when they closed, people must have said, "Wheeling who?" It was not so much its size (WDCO had as many as 120 employees) as it was community awareness. We'll speak more about this later.

For the sake of clarity, we have chosen to differentiate "artists," "decorators," and "skilled technicians." Our definition of an artist is someone who had the skills and the freedom to develop new designs for the business. A decorator, also being very talented, is an individual who takes a developed design, places it (or part of it) onto a blank piece of china or glassware, and then uses free-hand skills to add color or other embellishments. A decorator could be responsible for affixing the whole design or only one step in the production of the finished product. The technician is an individual who is primarily involved in only one step of a repetitive process.

Allan Reed, in his book on Pickard China, continually emphasizes the artists who worked at Pickard. Many of these individuals developed designs which became their own specialties (reference 3 in Bibliography). The most popular designs had more than one artist or decorator working on their production. Reed leaves the impression that if you signed your work you were probably more of an artist than a decorator, whether you designed the work or not. Reed's book gives large listings of the various artists by the years during which they were working at Pickard. Many of the non-product photographs in the book show individual artists or groupings of artists. The outdoor group photographs lend a feeling of a certain degree of familiarity, comradery, and esprit de corps.

As for WDCO, the artists and/or decorators as a general rule did not sign their work. We have found only three exceptions. The first was a small three-handled bowl (1.6" high and 6.3" in diameter) with a Royal Epiag Czechoslovakia glazed stamp, a Wheeling kiln-fired trademark, and the name of Bessie C. Fritz, signed in gold. This certainly does look like a signed piece. There is one problem though; none of the former employees of WDCO whom we have talked to seem to have ever heard of a Bessie Fritz. Of course, it could be that Bessie Fritz worked for the china manufacturer and not the decorator. Again, a lack of records from WDCO

The scripted "Ransom" signature.

is a major hindrance in all of this analysis.

One might reason that the china items were not decorator-signed because it would take extra time and might even require an additional firing. The item had to be turned over, a brush dipped in gold paint, and then the signature applied. The only problem with this is that about 90 percent of the china and pottery items decorated by WDCO have a gold number on the bottom of them that was hand-applied. These numbers showed from which company the blank had been purchased. It appears that some of the time a company had more than one number assigned to it and the hand-painted gold numbers were used for different types of china items. On most though, the number seems to represent the manufacturing company.

The second exception to WDCO signatures on its products is the gold-signed signature "Ransom," (pictured above). This appears on a number of china pieces but there is never a number associated with the Ransom signature. The Ransom signature is variable in design, showing that it was applied by a number of different people. A 1950 WDCO, fiftieth anniversary brochure shows three pages of all-over-gold items (see pages 25 – 27). Most of these items are named (vase, coffee pot, etc.) and the ad includes the "number" of the manufacturer of the blank item. The exceptions are the items marked with no number, just the name "Ransom." One would assume that the Ransom name was just substituted for the company number. The Ransom name is on some of the earliest pieces (prior to 1920) of WDCO china. Yet, in the 1950 brochure, the Ransom name is still in use. We tried several approaches in trying to ascertain what the Ransom name signifies. We thought it could be that it is in reference to Ransom China of Japan, though we have no knowledge of the age of that company. Because of the type of china that company produced, we discarded the idea. While we have never had a Ransom piece with a number on it, we do have an early Hutschenreuther marked piece that also has the Ransom script on it. Could it be that Ransom script is just an indica-

tion that the item was manufactured by Hutschenreuther? Certainly, the "Ranson" (with an "n") pattern was one used by Hutschenreuther. Was WDCO just making a small change in the nomenclature by going from "Ranson" to "Ransom?" In doing research on WDCO at the Wheeling Library, we casually picked up what appeared to be a part of a 1922 Warwick China brochure. It had been in a generalized glass/china folder. The brochure was touting the new, "Avon shape which reproduces faithfully, for the first time in American china, the popular imported design known as "Ranson." Sure enough, it looks like WDCO was buying "Avon Ranson" and marking it as "Ransom" after the item had been decorated (See Appendix H).

The pages of the 1950 brochure showed some of the china patterns and types that we own with "Ransom" on them. We conclude (for now) that early Ransom was Hutschenreuther (see the sugar and creamer from Plate 75), and the later Ransom was Warwick (creamer and sugar from Plate 74). The two pitchers in both photographs, though of different sizes, are probably from Warwick China.

A third group of signed items has only initials on the bottoms of the objects (see page 16). A quality comparison (they range from very poor to fairly good quality) makes one believe these items were probably used as training projects, teaching the individuals how to do the all-over-gold decorating. The novice decorators were probably allowed to take these non-saleable items home with them. Could it be that Bessie Fritz had signed, not initialed, her "final exam?" Until we can find more signed or initialed WDCO items we won't really be able to tell.

Various logos or trademarks were gold stamped or etched on the bottom of most of the WDCO china/porcelain/pottery. On some pieces there were no identifying marks at all. They are known to be Wheeling only by the design patterns used. In addition to the gold stamped or gold etched "marks," a sticker was attached to some items during World War II. One interesting WDCO plate we own has both a World War II sticker and a Hutschenreuther mark. We don't know if this was excess china that was carried forward into WWII, or if it was new material purchased just after WWII. After WWII, Wheeling decorated a number of items that were marked "Made in Occupied Japan." One such piece was made by Koran China and carried the mark "Wheeling Decorating Co.," along with number "35." This low number (some of the numbers are in the thousands) would probably indicate that this firm had been a source of blanks for some time.

We have found no marks on WDCO decorated glassware that would signify that the item was decorated by WDCO. Our guess would be that there had been some logo stickers on these items but they were removed by the purchaser as they detracted from the beauty of the design. There are also many WDCO items that contain a sticker showing the name of the firm or jeweler that sold the item. We know of no WDCO patterns that were used by another company, though other companies did use their own modifications of the WDCO patterns. The various WDCO marks or logos which are known at this time are shown in Chapter 4.

Good sources of information about WDCO, through the teens and up through the time they quit business, were the trade journals and the various glass trade shows. The Pittsburgh trade show was probably the most important trade show for WDCO, but other metropolitan areas like New York City and Chicago had them also. Naturally, with its location about 60 miles north of Wheeling, the Pittsburgh trade show had a special appeal. The *Crockery and Glass Journal* was probably the most important trade journal to the glass business. (Reference 4 in Bibliography). It was so important that it was published weekly up to 1928. From a historical point of view, the trade journals help tell approximately when many of the WDCO designs were released. They also gave a history of various sales representatives WDCO used. All of the passages listed below were taken from the pages of the *Crockery and Glass Journal*. Several of the citations do not have identified weeks and page numbers.

March 1923, page 27 — From the Chicago Market Section — "Butcher and Forline have opened a large and attractive permanent display in the Heyworth Building, 29 E. Madison Street, where they will show samples from the Wheeling Decorative Co. Liberty Glass Works, and the Crescent Glass Co. T. H. Butcher is well known to the trade of the middle-west, having covered that territory for a number of years. C. M. Forline was formerly the china and glassware buyer for Rike-Kumler Co. of Dayton, O., where he directed the work of the department for five years. The permanent exhibit is located in room 302 Heyworth Bldg."

February 1924, page 29 — From the Glass Factory Activities and Pittsburgh News — "Spiral optic blown stemware is being made a leading feature in the line of the Wheeling Decorating Co. this season, and it has proved to be a popular addition to the extensive offerings of this concern. The line is to be had in a gold encrusted band treatment. The variety of service plates offered by the Wheeling Decorating Co. this year is the largest ever assembled, and the variety of treatments has made the line an attractive one with the trade."

1924 — A 3.5" x 4.5" ad showing WDCO decoration No. 51 and the following information — "WHEELING DECORATING CO., WHEELING, W. VA. — Gold Encrusted and Hand Painted — CHINA AND GLASSWARE" – the following Sales representatives and their locations are listed: 1) SILVERBERG, 2 East 23rd St., New York, 2) THOS. H. BUTCHER, Chicago, 3) L. S. FITEMAN, 404 W. Baltimore St., Baltimore, 4) E. M. BARTLETT, 329 San Fernando Bldg., Los Angeles, Cal., 5) JULIAN GOLDBERG, 108 N. Queen St., Durham, N. C., and 6) R. D. OTTO, Road Representative.

September 1929 — A 3.5" x 4.75" ad showing Decoration No. 77, Cobalt, and the following information — "Decorated China and Glassware, Many new

Test items that have signed initials on the bottoms. The two outside creamers are signed "S.M.M." and the center one is signed "G.L.C." A salt and pepper set in Plate 138 has "G.L.C." '57 also.

creations now ready for your approval, Wheeling Decorating Co." — In the sales representatives listing, the Butcher and the Fiteman organizations were no longer showing WDCO items. The following two were added: 1) GEORGE TURNER, Middle West, 17 N. Wabash Ave., Chicago, and 2) CANADIAN CUT GLASS CO., Winnipeg, Canada.

December 1930, page 143 — A 4.75" x 7" ad showing four items, a) a plate with Decoration No. 100 (information in the WDCO design book says "no etching, print only"), b) a six-sided short vase of almost equal height and width, though unclear, probably all-over-gold Decoration No. 11, c) a squat, black glass lidded candy dish with unclear pattern, and d) a large shot glass with a somewhat comical polo player, design pattern unknown. The text of the ad reads, "DECORATED CHINA AND GLASSWARE — Many new creations now ready for your approval. — WHEELING DECORATING CO. — Wheeling W. Va. — LINE ON DISPLAY AT PITTSBURGH SHOW — ROOMS 343-344 FORT PITT HOTEL." In the sales representatives listing, George Turner was replaced by J. W. Bakster, Inc., 1509 Merchandise Mart, Chicago, Ill., and Silverberg was replaced by J. Walter Green, 200 Fifth Ave., rm. 551, New York.

February 1931 — This appears to be an editorial page with a 2.75" x 3.25" display. All items shown are of the same design, which appears to be a hunting scene with a horse, rider, and trees. This is an unnumbered design but a steel etching plate copy may be similar to the display ad. The text copy for this ad, which must have been published right after the annual trade show, reads, "A Cocktail Ensemble —The latest Wheeling Decorating Co. Creation. The Pittsburgh display of the Wheeling Decorating Co., Wheeling, W. Va. was filled with surprises this year. One of the most outstanding of these was a cocktail ensemble, an original creation with this concern, consisting of six old-fashioned cocktail glasses, a two-handled canapé tray, relish dish with three divisions for olives, salted nuts, etc. and an ice bucket. The set makes a complete and most unusual equipment for liquid refreshment. One of its attractive features is the charmingly appropriate decorations in which the ensemble may be had. At present there are five decorative treatments, four of which have interesting scenes done in brightly colored enamels and gold and are called: Coaching, Golfing, Hunting, and Fox Hunting. The latter comes in six different scenes, one for each cocktail glass in the ensemble. The rims of the glasses are edged in coin gold. The other decoration, which is somewhat modern in feeling, is called Rainbow. It has enamel bands of blue, red, green, and yellow, in graduating widths from the edge of the pieces to the center, giving a most colorful, spiral effect. Beaker-shaped glass and highballs and a cocktail shaker may also be had to match the ensemble in any of the decorations mentioned. The entire line,

including other new creations, is on display with the firm's New York representative, J. Walter Green, in Room 551 in the Fifth Avenue Building." Note, the Rainbow pattern, Golfer pattern and a "Pointing" Dog pattern are all shown on a page in Knoblich's design book, but without any design numbers.

June 1936 — An editorial type of page with a 3" x 2.5" display of three decorated glasses says, "The sportsman and 'would be' sportsman will want to stock up on the new tumblers from Wheeling Decorating Co. now at J. Walter Green. Hand-painted hunt scenes, a variety of game, or several species of fish are colorfully depicted on clear crystal. These are seen in a complete range of sizes, with or without a gold traced rim." Note, though not identical to the scenes shown with the ad, there were several other fish and wildlife scenes shown in Design numbers 301 to 304.

A business directory showed that in 1951, WDCO had sales offices located with J. Walter Green in New York, Gillard Sales in Wabasso, Minnesota, with the Walter Hovey Co. of San Francisco, California, and with Julian Goldberg of Durham, North Carolina. By 1952, Mrs. E. D. Leavitt, 1522 Merchandise Mart, Chicago, Illinois, had also been added. Thus, it would appear that within the decorated china and glassware business there were significant turnovers of the representatives who displayed and showed WDCO products. Only Julian Goldberg had been with WDCO from 1924 until 1952.

Albert Knoblich also said that at one time there were sales representatives in South Africa and in Germany, but he does not remember who these individuals were. In a review article from the 1994 second West Virginia Glass Festival, held August 5 – 7, at the Oglebay Institute Glass Museum in Wheeling, it states: "During its peak years, the Wheeling Decorating Co. was a financial gold mine. In fact, with sets of china selling for $1,500 or more, one of the company's salesmen made more than $100,000 a year in commissions during the 1920s." One must remember that those were the pre-Depression years, and the overall economy of the U. S. was at a very high level during that part of the 1920s.

We have no idea how these business representatives operated with WDCO. Did they forward orders back to WDCO or did they fill orders from what they had on consignment from WDCO? The latter would involve double packaging and shipping, so this does not seem too practical. The only indication we have about the business transactions of Wheeling are three requests for shipment that had been stuck in the design book. The first was a request for ⅙ dozen cups and saucers from A. S. Pflueger, Jeweler, in Roanoke, Virginia. Someone had penciled in the word "tea" in front of the word "cups." The note included, "Ship at once via best way," and was dated January 10, 1936. It looks like there was another note added up in the right-hand corner that said, "All C," probably meaning "all china." This may have indicated a method of shipping or packaging. The second order had 25 different items, with the items being listed by their source number (blank manufacturer) and the type of the item ordered. This list is shown here. One of the lines reads "⅙ dozen 1253 Coffee Pot." The largest line order reads "½ dozen 543 Bon Bon." The total number of items or sets was 85 or so. This order was dated October 18, but gave no year. It had been placed by Stern Bros., 41, 42nd St., New York, N.Y. There are several checkmarks on the order form, suggesting it may have been used as a packing list. Three of the items ordered have the typed notation "ENCR 11" to the far right of the item ordered. We have no idea what this means. Two of the items beside the number are sugar and creamers, while the third is a large vase. WDCO Design No. 11 is the most popular all-over-gold pattern showing "Doves, Roses, and Daisies." While the ENCR 11 could imply that was the desired design pattern, most of the other items on the list were made in the famous D-11 design also. That was probably the only pattern used with many of them. Still, maybe the ENCR 11 stands for encrusted 11 and on these particular items there may have been another pattern choice.

Packing list for shipping to the Stern Bros. in New York.

One last point on the Stern Bros. order. In the upper right corner there was a line drawn through a sentence that says, "CONFIRMATION TO ____." The question is who got the confirmation? J. W. Green was the New York sales representative for WDCO, at least from 1930 to 1952. Could his name be there? While the length of the unknown name is about right and the first letter looks like it could be a "J," conclusive confirmation that the name even starts with a "J" would be hard to assure. If it is J. W. Green, that would certainly give clearer evidence as to how WDCO and the sales representatives operated.

The final order letter (page 19) says at the top, "CHARGE J. W. GREEN." We assume that means to credit J. W. Green with this sale. Under this, the note says "ship to Mrs. E. J. Gorman, 33 Kingsbury Road, New Rochelle, N. Y." It is dated only with June 12. The body of the order says "¹⁄₁₂ Doz. 811 Coffee Set." Farther along the same line it reads "182 Red" and

beside that what appears to be the handwritten letters, "A. D." and then a checkmark. We believe the "182" refers to Design 182. This pattern in the design book calls for bands of platinum and black enamel on an item. Our guess is that the "Red" means that the black bands are to be replaced with red enamel. We have no idea of what the added "A.D." stands for. It could be a simple notation for something like "Already Done." The next line appears to be a summary of the transaction and reads, "One Coffee Pot, Sugar & Cream, & 6 Cups & Saucers." Below all of this is a sketch with bands on a "Pot" and a "Sugar," more indications that the field representatives sent orders directly to WDCO for filling and shipping. We have no indications that any stores were carrying significant amounts of open-stock of WDCO items.

Another item we know that WDCO had was a glass cutting machine. This machine used various diamond coated wheels to cut a repeated pattern in a glass item. Albert Knoblich, Karl's son, said that he seldom saw the machine being used when he was in the WDCO building in the late 1930s and 1940s. We do know that in the 1940s and 1950s some of the WDCO machine-cut glass work was contracted to the Sickles Cutting Shop, across the Ohio River from Wheeling, in Bellaire, Ohio. Still, we do have a small WDCO sherbet glass that has a

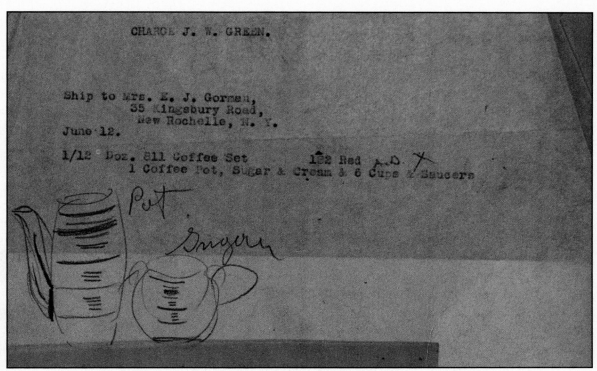

An order for a single coffee service.

half-inch wide etched (design No. D-2a, Minton), gold coated band on the top, and a thin gold band on the base. This sherbet has a machine-cut pattern, under the half-inch gold band. This pattern consists of five, six-leafed flowers, all with open centers (see Plates 14 and 15). The flowers are connected by a thin vine with a small leaf and by a long fern leaf (or wheat stem) that goes almost all the way between each flower. Underneath the flowers, vine, and fern leaf are a series of what would appear to be short spears but which were probably designed as leaves with various lengths of stems. It is all very elegant. Much to our surprise, this sherbet had been given by my mother to my daughter Laura Marshall 15 years ago in Oklahoma. I had grown up with it in my home and did not make the connection until I saw it. Two other machine-cut items are shown in Plates 484 and 485. While we cannot totally verify that these are WDCO cut items, the indications are that they were done by Wheeling. One small indication comes from the fact that Wheeling decorated large amounts of Candlewick with gold. The only items we have seen with this cut pattern have all been on gold decorated Candlewick.

As WDCO moved into the late 1920s and 1930s, we were able to gain information about the company through interviews with employees who had worked at Wheeling Decorating. Ms. Olive Muegge, on the right, was one such employee. She was born in Wheeling in 1909 of German descent. She began working at WDCO in 1925 when she

was 16 and stayed with the company until 1942. Her brother, Bill Muegge, later became the mayor of Wheeling. She walked to work each morning as she lived only a half block away from the WDCO building at 700 Market Street. She remembers that Frank Thurm, the originator of the business, was seldom out in the working area and had little direct contact with the average worker. She considered him to be a very wealthy man. Thurm owned the house at 704 Market Street which he rented out for many years to a McKeever family. She also remembered Oliver Crumley, who was the bookkeeper while she was there, and that he became the last president of the company. Olive worked in the pattern department, which was

On the left, Mary Etta Norman, daughter of Leland Taylor, WDCO president from 1949 – 1957. On the right, Ms. Olive Muegge, currently 93 years old. She worked at WDCO from 1925 – 1942.

A German postcard showing Frank and Carrie Thurm touring the country. Probably from the 1920s.

supervised by Elmer Shire, and it had about 15 employees. She would often babysit in the evenings for the Shires' two little boys. The pattern department was where decorative design patterns were transferred to blank china items before they were sent to an etching or enameling area. Her third floor work area, which was above the main office, was entered by a set of stairs on the outside of the building. She sat facing front windows which provided a lot of light for doing the necessary detail work of the pattern department. Beyond her work area was a small room where shipping and packing were supervised and done by Lee Taylor. Lee later became the second president of WDCO. Items came to Muegge's department from the warehouse, farther to the back of the building. She remembers

Karl Knoblich playing the zither and Walter Rupel with the violin. Late teens to early 1920s.

Ducks hand painted on heavy blue cellophane. Used as salesman's samples.

great stacks of china being brought to her and one day a man fell carrying a stack of plates. Mr. Knoblich, the chief designer-artist, called out, "How many did you break?"

Olive described her work group, mostly women, as a "bunch of teenagers having fun." In October, the Christmas business would pick up, and they had to work overtime to get the rush orders filled. The group of girls she worked with would go to her house and share dinner during the rush times and then go back to work. Ms. Muegge remembers the time she and her workmates vacationed together at Chippaway Lake, a nearby resort. There they rented a cottage, spent the weekend, and did lots of boating out on the lake. Each employee got one to two weeks of vacation time, depending on how long they had worked for WDCO. Social activities were a big part of the interactions at WDCO. She recalls dances being held almost every night at the Firemen's Hall. As a sign-of-the-times, she remembers her grandfather belonged to the Beethoven society, which was a beer/singing club. Music appears to have been an important item at these times. Page 20 shows Karl Knoblich playing the zither and Walter Rupel (artist/decorator) holding a violin, in a sitting room atmosphere.

One of the nice events that Ms. Muegge remembers was an order coming in around 1940 from Mrs. Franklin Roosevelt for a 100-piece set of china. The Roosevelts had specified German Bavarian China, so china made by Hutschenreuther was used. It was a pattern that she remembers as being cobalt blue and containing an inside band of small tulips. Mr. Knoblich used his own secret formula for the cobalt blue and he always prepared it in the basement of his home. Ms. Muegge believes the china service was for the White House, though it could have been for the Roosevelt's Hyde Park residence. It appears that the design pattern she was referring to was a complex pattern in that it contains other patterns within it. The pattern starts with a narrow outer band (⅛") of small flowers, with these resembling a very fine gold necklace (D-36). Then there is a band of cobalt blue, possibly 2" wide, on a dinner plate. Finally, on the inside of the cobalt, the design contains a repeating tulip pattern (⅝" wide), with the tulips separated by narrow solid bars with dots over them. This tulip band is shown as the D-46a pattern. Plate 280 shows the D-36 and D-46a borders and it is similar to the Roosevelt's set, but the checkered flag design was replaced with the wide cobalt blue band. It is interesting to note WDCO also did a church plate with the design of the Hyde Park Community Church on it.

As the years progressed, the changes in public tastes and styles can be seen by the varying patterns used by WDCO. The very earliest designs were very formal and regal. They were not only beautiful, but

breathtaking. A classic example is seen in design D-47 (Plates 217 through 222), with leaves and fruit combined with geometric patterns. Around 1930, the pattern choices were changing towards less formality and more free flowing designs. The new patterns in this era called for more hand-painted enamel and less gold. Roses were one of the most favored subjects. This gave a somewhat more delicate air to the layout. As an example, the D-125a design (starting with Plate 323) has a small Greek Key border outside a gentle band of rosebuds and leaves which are connected by a double vine.

In addition, the 1930s brought increased emphasis to the light-hearted designs such as sporting and athletic activities. One example of this was a set of Guardsman Cocktail glasses purchased by Queen Elizabeth's mother in New York City. They were sold by Walter Green, the New York sales representative. These designs were taken, with permission, from the well known Schenley Whiskey ads of the era.

Various bird glasses were a theme in the mid-to-late 1930s. Albert Knoblich has a set of the bird designs, used by salesmen, that were on heavy cellophane. That way a salesman would not have to carry the actual glasses into the sales territory. Two of these are shown on page 20. Most of the bird items at this time were true depictions of the birds, much as would be found in a bird book. There was at least one set of birds that had an international flavor containing a Java, a Red Billed Weaver, a Bul Bul, and others. In the early 1940s WDCO expanded the bird theme by painting bird figures that were almost three dimensional. This process was developed by WDCO artist Vincent Beck (see page 42). Though he did not know the process, he had seen a similar technique in Bavaria, so he set about to develop this layered or raised paste process. This technique involved laying down one layer of colored enamel on a glass blank, kiln drying it, and then repeating the process until the raised design was finished. This often required four passes through the kiln. The raised birds were shaped by using dental tools. Albert Knoblich remembers going along on a trip to Beaver Falls, Pennsylvania, in 1942 to buy needed paste supplies from a paint factory. Much of this special enamel still ended up being imported from Europe. These raised birds appear to be unique but we don't know if other firms tried this laborious process or not. Nor do we know if designs other than birds were produced in the raised pattern. We do believe that Beck also did a raised flower series on glasses but they could have been "singular" or research type items. In the mid- to late 1940s, WDCO was doing more of the routine type glassware decorating. This included rubber stamps and decal transfer patterns and was directed at higher volume and less expensive applications. We do know they did contracting work with Cambridge Glass and Duncan Miller.

Mixed in with all of this was the continued production of the all-over-gold china and pottery. Nothing prevented WDCO from going back and pulling up an older etching when a need or request was made. There were always special requests to put someone's home or church on a collection of china. Karl Knoblich hand engraved many of these designs into steel plates. Church plates must have been a fairly good business for WDCO, but probably moreso after photoengraving became commonplace. One of the early surprises in the research for this book occurred when stepdaughter Kelly Norman, in Barboursville, WV, turned over a borrowed church plate and discovered it was decorated by WDCO. The photo below is a snapshot of this china at her church. It is still in good condition. We also have a Barboursville High School 25th anniversary plate (1927-1952) that was probably produced about the same time as the church china service.

There were lots of college, military, and other organizations that wanted their crest or insignia on some item of glass or china. Since the organizations were the owners of the designs, it is hard to verify which ones were done by WDCO and which were done by other firms. The only way to be sure is to see a WDCO trademark on the item.

All in all, the design tastes of the people changed dramatically over the life of WDCO. The designs had started out with a mostly traditional classic flair, with some inclusion of the undulating and curving lines of the Art Nouveau period. This changed from the elegant gold of the teens, to the Art Deco of the 1920s and 1930s. The dramatic style of the Art Deco period, with its very bold colors and geometric designs, showed up as patterned swirls of color on glassware and even Egyptian motifs. Certainly the Flapper era of the 1920s and early 1930s showed a disdain for the more conventional forms of decoration. The late 1930s and early 1940s maintained somewhat of a status quo with the effects of the Depression and the World War weighing on peoples' desires for change. For WDCO, the post-war years forced a practicality on them. While they could still make and deliver their classic designs, the specter of public mass commercialization forced them towards lower profit items while still using their expensive talent and equipment. This, along with a general demise in the glass/china industry, caused WDCO to reevaluate how and with whom they were doing business. Then a leadership change at WDCO heightened these concerns.

In late 1945 and into 1946, Frank Thurm and Karl Knoblich began having a "falling out." Karl, as production foreman, had apparently authorized the work force to once again use the large, diamond shaped gold logo to cover the country of manufacture on purchased blanks. Since the country was just coming out of war, this may have been an attempt to play down the names of the countries we had been fighting against. Or maybe it happened before the war was over and they were using china that had been purchased before the war. It had been against the law to do this for many years but it may have just been an expedient measure to help get over the realities of the war years. Regardless, the U. S. Customs Service informed WDCO that it was going to be fined for this action. Karl evidently had a silent partnership in WDCO and reportedly Mr. Thurm asked Karl to give up this partnership in exchange for Mr. Thurm paying the fine himself. The fine was thought to be several thousand dollars, but later it was suggested to be more in the range of $300. The two men were quickly at odds over this whole episode and Karl, who was also WDCO's head designer, artist, and engraver, considered getting another job. Karl certainly was the creative force behind the success of the WDCO business, and it is known that he was in contact with others as far as other employment opportunities were concerned. Years earlier Karl had received other offers of work but he had felt that since Mr. Thurm was 20 years older than he, his best potential lay in staying with WDCO (See Appendix G). While Karl was thinking about leaving WDCO in 1946, this never came about because he became ill with cancer and died at the age of 60 in March of 1948. Albert reports that his dad did little work in 1947. Thirteen months later, Mr. Thurm was also dead at the age of 80. These two deaths eliminated the production and financial leaders of WDCO. The future of the company was now

Non-pictorial church plates by WDCO. These items have probably been in service for more than 45 years. They still look good.

James Leland ("Lee") Taylor, 1900 – 1957. Lee Taylor replaced Frank Thurm in the leadership role in 1949 when he became president of WDCO.

left in the hands of other employees.

The Concluding Years 1948 – 1962

With the deaths of Frank Thurm and Karl Knoblich, the ownership of WDCO passed to three employees: Lee Taylor, salesman; Oliver Crumley, business manager; and Walter Rupel, artist and decorator. We don't know if this succession arrangement had been set up by Mr. Thurm before he died or if these three individuals organized themselves to buy out the business from Mrs. Thurm. A "Memorandum of Agreement" dated October 31, 1950, indicates that Mrs. Thurm sold the tract of land at Seventh and Market to Lee Taylor and Walter Rupel for $15,000. A second document, "Summary of the Contemplated Sale in the Matter of the Wheeling Decorating Company" showed that the selling of the business proper came to an additional amount of $50,000. Oliver Crumley appears to have been a one-third partner in this sale. The sale involved $15,000 for the building and $35,000 worth of stock, with the terms of payment being spelled out. The undated newspaper article in Appendix C states, "The business has been in operation for the past 51 years, being incorporated for the past two years." Thus, the stock had probably been issued with the incorporation of WDCO. We don't know if, at that time, others had shares of stock also.

The choice of people to own and run the new corporation seems to have been a good one. Walter Rupel, with skills as a decorator, could help keep the artistic aspect of the business in good shape. Oliver Crumley, who had worked in the front office, could look after the purchasing, sales, and general accounting part of the business. But the man chosen to be president of WDCO, Lee Taylor, had a background that tied the whole of the system together. James Leland Taylor was born in 1900 in Hendrysburg, Ohio. He graduated from high school there, after which he attended and graduated from the Elliott School of Business in Wheeling. When graduated he started work at WDCO as an office boy. Mr. Thurm liked what he saw in Lee and very quickly put him in charge of the shipping department. In a very few years he also became a salesman, primarily handling accounts in nearby cities. Mr. Taylor quickly developed an appreciation for the entire business, though he never did any of the artistic decorating. He did know the ins and outs of how everything was done and was aware of both economic and operational concerns with the business.

The WDCO had as many as 120 employees at times, and even in the middle of the Depression in 1936 there were 80 workers. By 1951, there were only 40 people at WDCO. This speaks not so much about hard times but to the way of doing business. Production rates of 60 dozen items per day suggest some significant level of utilitarian ware was being produced. Many of the items were fancy glasses but were probably decal transfer decorated. There were a very large number of competitors in this type business. Federal Glass, Anchor Hocking, and Libby Glass all produced various types of bird glasses, usually decorated by transfer processing. Still, WDCO gold-coated china, hand-decorated birds on glasses, and various types of bar ware helped maintain an artistic base to the business.

A 50-year celebration was held by WDCO in 1950. Little is known about this event other than the brochure that was published. This four-page document is shown on pages 24 – 27. The quality of this brochure is only fair. As the name on the brochure suggests, only all-over-gold items were shown. There may have been a separate price list but this has not been found. Note again the "Ransom" (Warwick China?) items displayed.

In May of 1956, Lee Taylor had a radio interview with a local station, WWVA of Wheeling (See Appendix B.). Lee explained the operation at WDCO and noted that they did very little sales business in Wheeling. He stated that the local department and jewelry stores, "— don't patronize our home products very much." He also said, "— I would say there isn't one out of a thousand knows this place is here in Wheeling, although it has been here 55 years." As an aside, Mr. Taylor erroneously stated later in the interview that the business was started in 1913, which would have made the business only 43 years old in 1956. When asked where all the glasses went, Lee responded, "Well, they go to nearly all the better jewelry stores all over the United States."

In the interview, Mr. Taylor pointed out an important technology change in the way designs were produced. Photographs of a church or college seal, for example, could be taken and transferred to lithographic stone, probably by a photoengraving process. Thus, the tedious process of hand-engraving metal plates could be by-passed. Copies could then be transferred from the lithographic stone and placed on the item to be decorated.

When asked by the interviewer how the business was doing in 1956, Lee responded that with it being an election year, business was not as good as 1955 which had been a record year. He said he always found business to be off a little in presidential election years.

There were no indications that WDCO was in any kind of downturn in the 1955 – 1957 time period. But from this time on, age factors became a big problem for

WHEELING GOLD

CHINA

50th

ANNIVERSARY

1900   1950

WHEELING DECORATING CO., Inc.

Wheeling, West Virginia

1950 WDCO brochure, cover.

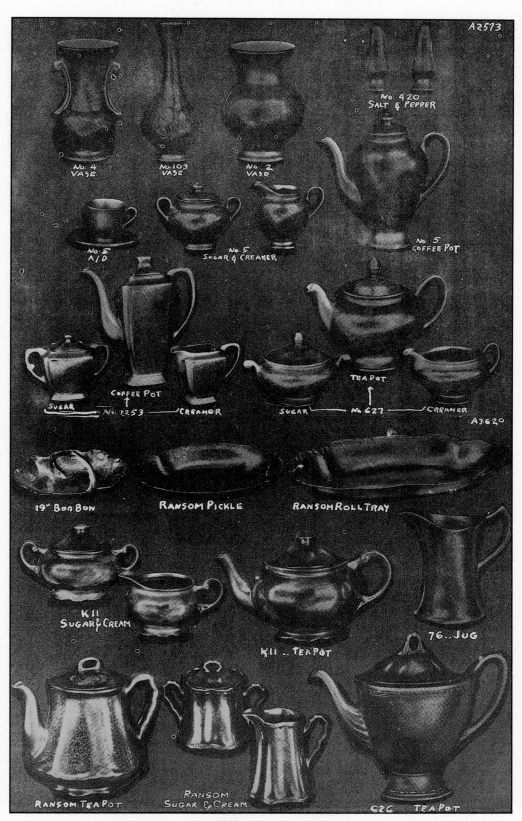

1950 WDCO brochure, page 2.

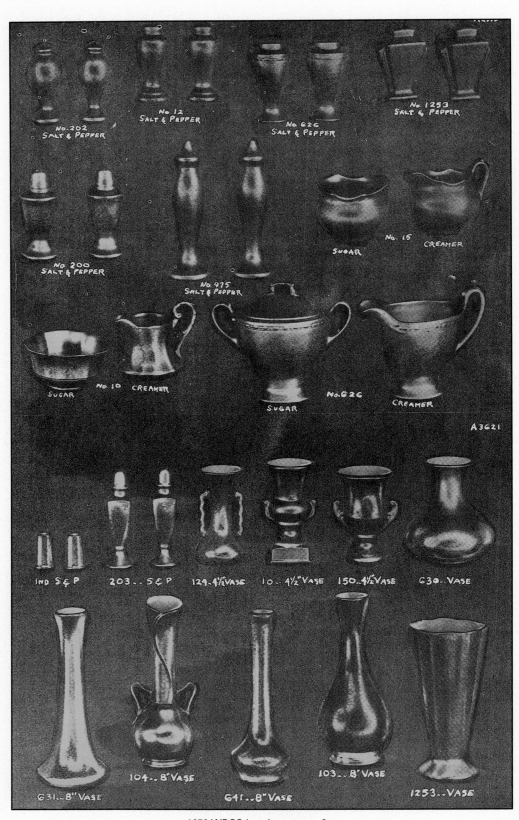

1950 WDCO brochure, page 3.

PRICES SUBJECT TO CHANGE WITHOUT NOTICE

REGULAR PACKAGE CHARGE F. O. B. WHEELING, W. VA.

1950 WDCO brochure, page 4.

Oliver Crumley, 1905 – 1972. President of WDCO from 1957 – 1962.

Oliver and Irene Crumley on their wedding day in 1948.

WDCO. Several of the few remaining artists were in their mid-seventies. The distributors around the country who had been very loyal to WDCO were also faced with this problem. Many of these distributors were run by very knowledgeable but single proprietors. Thus, WDCO faced major problems. The only person in WDCO who really had the necessary grasp of the entire operation was Leland Taylor. Tragically, Mr. Taylor suddenly passed away in May of 1957. Lee certainly had a foretelling of what was to come with the business if he were not available to coordinate its activities. Upon his death a note was found in his billfold that said to sell all of his stock in the business as soon as possible.

There is not much information available about WDCO over its last five years of existence. It is known that Oliver Crumley became the last president of WDCO. Walter Rupel retired. J. Walter Green, the New York sales representative, became ill and quit the business. Julian Goldberg, the Durham, North Carolina representative, retired. And on and on it went with others closing their businesses or retiring. While aging people were a big part of the problem, the desire for hand-decorated or gold-encrusted dinnerware was rapidly diminishing. WDCO really was just falling in line with much of the rest of the "elegant glass" industry. Cambridge Glass Co. had closed in 1959, Dunbar Glass Co. (WDCO used their barware items) closed in 1953, Heisey Glass closed in 1957, Paden City Glass Co. closed in 1951, and the Tiffin Glass Co. was bought by employees in 1963, then changed hands a cou-

ple of times over the next six years.

We had interviews with Oliver Crumley's wife, Irene, who also worked at WDCO as a decorator. She and Oliver's 1948 wedding picture is shown above. We asked her if she could remember what happened over WDCO's last few years. She felt that was a little funny because she had spent many years trying to forget the demise of the company. She said at the end there were only three employees, including her husband and herself, and the number of orders became so small that they would only work a day or two a week.

Irene had started work at WDCO in 1941 and she locked the door for the last time in 1962. She had married Oliver in 1948. Oliver had started work at Wheeling at a very young age and became Frank Thurm's right-hand man. He handled dictation, typing, timekeeping, bookkeeping, pay master, and whatever else needed doing. He attended trade shows, set up displays, and informed the tradespeople and agents about WDCO.

With Thurm's death in 1949, the new corporation bought back Mrs. Thurm's stock, then Lee Taylor's stock was purchased in 1957, and finally, when Walter Rupel retired, his stock was repurchased. This drastically depleted the companies' working capital. It rapidly became necessary for the employees to seek work elsewhere. In an effort to survive, Oliver became the printer, the waxer, the etcher, and kiln firer, as did Irene. Irene even had a workshop in their basement where she could work on items at night, then take them in to be kiln fired the next morning.

Since they had three children in school, it became necessary for Oliver to take another job. He became manager of a Mary Carter Paint store. Irene tried to keep the business afloat but one day she received an extremely large bill from the gas company which they could not pay. Thus, the gas was shut off, the bank foreclosed their loan on the property, and the Wheeling Decorating Company was no more. Irene said it was a very sad day and one that she has tried to forget in spite of the many happy and rewarding times. To state it fairly, good and bad, it was a massive part of her family's life.

Why had WDCO gone the way of the other glass and decorating companies in the area? Certainly, as stated above, changing tastes and the aging of the support people played an important role. Perhaps another factor was the technology and skill capabilities of WDCO. Its equipment was too dated, its technology was too precise, and maybe, just maybe, they were living in the past. They could not move out of their heyday of the 1920s and 1930s.

Why would we suggest this? A fairly simple example supports at least part of this. A new company opened up in Wheeling while WDCO was still in operation. It was Conrad Crafters. We talked to Carolyn Conrad about this business. She and three others were working at the Warwick plant when it started closing in 1951. Warwick was in the middle of two large production runs for other companies. They had already made the china but it needed to be decorated. So these four people were asked, and Conrad Crafters was started with a year of pre-dedicated work. This work was primarily decal transfer and gold band guilding. Coffee cups, state commemorative plates, and church plates were some of the many items they undertook after they finished their commitment to the two large companies. No etched, gold-coated items. No hand-painted enameled flowers. They stuck to their business of the times, knowing both their capabilities and their limitations. They are still in business today. Yes, it is just possible that WDCO had a difficult time moving out of the past and into the realities of the present.

Chapter 3: *Decorating Operations*

We find it necessary to explain how the essential decorating operations at WDCO were performed. One of the main reasons for doing this is to show the complexity of the processes used to create the beautiful gold and enameled products. The understanding of the techniques and equipment used for the production of these elaborate decorations adds not only a sense of history but also a sense of the "value-adding" characteristics of the craftspeople and their skills. As stated in the previous chapter, this complexity may have also helped lead to the closing of the Wheeling Decorating Company.

The design and decorating operations covered in this chapter were those carried out at the business location at 700 Market Street (Market and Seventh) in Wheeling, West Virginia. We have only speculation and limited information on what took place during the years before the business completed its move to the Market Street address. At that time, 1900, the business was located in an old clubhouse at the intersection of Mount Wood and National Road. The conclusion can be drawn that the business had at least one small kiln which allowed for the firing of the hand enameled blanks. Since glassware decorating, at that time, had not reached a great popularity, it is assumed that the bulk of the decorating was done on china, porcelain, or pottery. This is further verified by the fact that 25 years ago Albert Knoblich (the lead designer's son) remembers seeing a plate in an antique store that was marked "Frank Thurm China Co. Whg. W. Va." However, one 1952 article by a natural gas supplier said that Frank Thurm's and Robert Engelhardt's first products were decorative paperweights and lamp shades.

The 1903 – 1904 business directory for the city of Wheeling shows the name of the business was the Wheeling Decorating Company and it was located at 700 Market Street. At some point before WDCO took over the facilities at this address, it had been the Kenny Brewery Building. The description of the building and equipment is based on the recollections of Albert Knoblich and thus shows what the facilities were like in the mid-1930s and 1940s. We will describe the various locations, and their related activities within the building, as if an individual were standing across the street looking at the front of the building at 700 Market Street.

Figure 1 shows the front of the WDCO building and the small house next to it. From this position, there appears to be three floors to the building with the first floor being painted brown. The building is only about

Figure 1. Wheeling Decorating Company property at Market and Seventh Streets, where the company began in 1904.

Figure 2. Entrance area to the WDCO second and third floors.

25 feet wide. A close look at the space between the two buildings in Figure 2 shows there is more of the WDCO structure behind the house at 704 Market. Going to the right of the small house (Figure 3), it can be seen that the WDCO building is more expansive than the front view would suggest. Figure 4, showing the far left side of the building, makes it clear that there are four levels in the building. The left side view shows that there is a very steep slope going uphill from Market Street. The front portion of the building (three stories) goes back 39 feet from the edge of the street. The back portion of the building, with the third and fourth story levels, goes back another 92 feet to the edge of West Chapline Street behind the WDCO buildings. Thus, the building has a straight-line depth of 131 feet, street to street. From this left side view a wall can be seen at the front of the building where Mr. Thurm once had a small garage for his car. When photographed, two cars were actually parked where the small garage was located. Figure 5 gives the upper view of the left side of the build-

Figure 3. Right side view of the third and fourth floors of WDCO. The south and west top floor windows provided light for the artists /decorators.

Figure 4. Left side view of the WDCO property. The incline up this hill limited the back section of the WDCO to only two floors.

Figure 5. Loading dock areas for shipping and receiving. The third floor loading dock area was below the bricked-up windows on the right.

Figure 6. Back property line on West Chapline Street. The acid/wax room is in the taller back portion of the building.

ing. A heating and refrigeration company, Mountain Aire, now uses the building. The open door is an entryway into the back of the building and the covered entryway was the location of a loading platform. Figure 6 shows the back of the building, with the taller portion to the far left being the location of the old acid etch room.

Looking again from the front of the building there used to be another house to the right of 704 Market,

and it was number 706 Market (there was no 702 Market). Both of these properties, 704 and 706 Market, were owned by Mr. Thurm and, as was noted earlier, the 704 address was rented to a McKeever family. The 700 and 704 buildings were separated by about six feet, with concrete steps in the open space. These steps led up to a second floor side entrance at the back of the buildings. From the landing of these concrete steps, a wooden stairway was attached to the side of

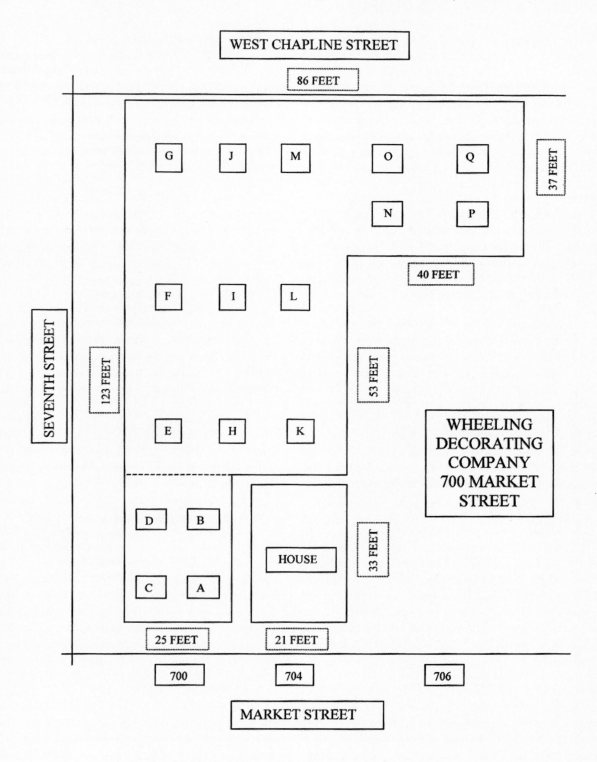

Schematic of the WDCO building floor plan.

the building and this led to the third floor. If you look closely at Figure 2, you can see some paint high on the wall. This paint says "OFFICE," and is enclosed by an arrow pointing to the left. This was where the wooden stairs stopped and where most employees entered the facilities. Behind the 704 house, and 39 feet from the edge of Market Street, the wall of the WDCO building was extended to the right behind the entire width of the house, it being only about 19 feet wide. The WDCO building then followed the same edge line as the right side of the 704 House and went towards the back of the property for about 52 feet. At that point the building turned right behind the 706 property for another 40 feet or so. Then the right side of the building was completed by going 38 feet to the back property line. In viewing the building, one would guess that the 25 foot wide by 33 foot deep, three-story Market Street section was built first. Later, a 90 foot deep addition was made to the building, running behind the front section of the building and the neighboring houses. Initially, the first three stories only went back about 40 feet from the edge of the street because of the steep hill. Later, the back building, with only third and fourth level floors, was added. To help understand the layout and operation of the Wheeling Decorating Company, a rough schematic of the floor plan of the total building is shown on page 31. Capital letters are used to show locations in the building where various activities took place.

Today, the front of the WDCO building is dark brown on the first floor, and light blue on the second and third levels. Between the second and third floors the name of the company was written across the front of the building. If one looks carefully, the last two letters (CO.) of the company name can still be seen on the right front edge of the building. On the brown colored first floor of the building, there are two doors facing Market Street. The door on the right opened into a room that contained the heating equipment for the buildings, a hot water heater, and maybe even a steam generator (We call this area 1A & 1B to show the location is on the first floor). Behind the door on the left there was a carved-out area that was known as the "cave"(1C & 1D). The brewery had stored its beer in this cave. The cave was dug into the sloping hillside and was used by WDCO to store excelsior. Excelsior is a packing material made from fine strands of curled wood shavings. The excelsior was purchased in the form of compressed bales and was a very good and light packing material for shipping fragile items like china and glassware.

The second floor shows four windows facing Market Street. Behind the two windows on the right (2A) was the business office and Mr. Thurm's office area. As one came up the outside concrete stairs on the right side of the building, there was a door into this office area. Behind the two left windows (2C), in a separate

room, there was a paint mixing machine. Leading out of the office area and the paint mixing machine area there were doors that led into an open space (2B &2D), where there was an inside stairway that led to the third floor. The only other item in this space behind the two front rooms was a trap door with a pulley and a rope to hoist bales of excelsior up from the "cave" below. The bale would be broken open and whatever amount of excelsior was needed would be carried up the stairs to the third floor.

When coming to work almost all of the workers climbed the outside stairs, between 700 and 704 Market, to reach the third floor. As the employees entered the third floor there was a time clock by the door (3H). Near this same location at the top of the stairs, there was a room that contained a glass cutting machine which was used to make decorative cuts on glassware (3K). This room was in the area behind the 704 Market Street house. In general, much of the preparation techniques were performed on the third floor while many of the finishing operations were done on the fourth floor. Looking at the third floor from the front of the building, there were again four windows. Behind the two windows on the right (3A & 3B) were storage bins for various glass and china blanks. Many of the storage bins in the building are still in use as parts storage areas for Mountain Aire. There was also a restroom farther back (3E), as well as the stairs that came up from the second floor (3B). Behind the two windows on the left was the gold formulation room (3C). This room was vented because of the hazardous nature of parts of this operation. Just behind the gold formulation room was the spray room or washroom (3D). All of these just described third floor facilities were in the original 25 foot by 33 foot building with no fourth floor above this area. In the newer portion of the building, just behind the washroom and near the restroom, there was an unpacking and packing area (3E) that extended along the left wall of the building. This is where shipments of glass and china were received and where finished products were prepared for shipping. This area extended almost to the back of the third floor and there was an access door to a loading dock (3F) so shipments could be delivered by wagon or truck. Looking at Figure 5 this dock was located under the bricked-up windows at the right of the picture. There was also a set of stairs by the unpacking area (3E) that connected the third and fourth floors. The third floor area, from the stairway over to the time clock and all along the back wall, was filled with more storage bins, both for china and glassware and for engraving plates (3I, 3J, 3L, & 3M).

The third floor area behind the 706 Market Street property was the printing room or the pattern department. This room contained two work areas. As will be discussed later, the first area, called the printing table

(3N & 3P), was where designs were transferred from engraving plates to tissue paper. Then, in the second work area (3O & 3Q), these designs on the tissue were transferred to china or glassware at what was called the pattern table. There were windows in both of these areas to allow good light to come into the room. Later in the history of WDCO, this is where printed transfer decals were also applied to the various blanks. There was also another stairwell in this area (starting behind 3Q) so the china and glassware could be moved up to the etching area, the decorators, or to the kilns, all on the fourth floor.

Standing at street level, in front of 700 Market, the fourth floor cannot be seen easily unless one looks between the building and the 704 house. If it could be seen from the front, the decorators work area on the fourth floor would start just above the middle two windows on the right (4E) and would continue behind the 704 and 706 Market Street properties. Thus, artists and decorators were located at just about all of the south and west windows of the fourth floor (4E, 4H, 4K, 4L, 4N, & 4P). There were windows all along this area so there would be good light for the craftspeople. For the most part, the better artists got the best lit locations and the technicians got the "not-so-good" positions. Karl Knoblich's work space was above the two windows on the left as you look at the building (4E). To the rear, behind Karl's work space and continuing along the outside left wall (between 4E & 4F), was the packing table area where items were prepared for shipment. From this area there was access to a second loading dock (between 4F & 4G). This is also where one of the stairways comes up from the third floor. Behind and to the right of Karl's work area were more storage bins for finished items and for the storage of the etching plates (4I). There was also a fourth floor restroom in this same area (between 4I & 4M). The last 30 feet at the rear of the building (4G, 4J, & 4M) contained an enclosed area where there were 20 or so kilns of various sizes. These kilns extended for about 40 feet across the back of the building, with at least six of them being glass kilns. The vents from the kilns extended up through the roof of the fourth floor to discharge the heated air into the atmosphere. There was a door on the right-hand side of the kiln room (at 4M) that opened into the area where the other stairway came up from the third floor. It was in this area along the back wall where the gold polishing table was located (4O). Farther to the right and in the building portion behind the 706 property was the acid room (4Q). This enclosed 15 foot by 15 foot space had a separate acid etch room and space for wax coating and wax removal.

All in all, the WDCO building was using about 6,700 square feet of operating space, and at its peak times had up to 120 employees. This made for a moderate-sized decorating business.

Before we start the discussion of the decorating processes, it is necessary to talk about the quality of the glassware and china that Wheeling Decorating was using and how it was handled. The first step in the process was to buy only from the very best producers of the blanks (undecorated china or glassware). As indicated earlier, Mr. Thurm felt that for china and porcelain, the very best products came from Germany. For this reason, a great many of these blanks were purchased from Hutschenreuther. During WWI, this source was cut off and Mr. Thurm had to loosen his standards and experiment with suppliers from Japan and the United States. After the War, WDCO went back to Hutschenreuther but they also looked for other German and European producers. They also searched to find quality U.S. producers, and the listing in Chapter 7 shows some of the many companies with which they dealt. The same thing happened during WWII, but both Japan and Europe were lost as a source of blanks for decorating. With very few exceptions, the sources of glassware were in the U.S. and those known are also included in the listings in Chapter 7.

When china or glass blanks arrived at the WDCO facilities, they were carefully checked for any defects (3E). They were examined for bubbles, chipping, scratches, mold defects, and so on. One obvious test was to see if plates would stack evenly, without any waves. If they passed these reviews, then the items were washed in the spray room (3D) and sent to storage bins (3A & 3B) until they were needed for decorating. Why were they so picky with the blanks they used? For one thing, decorating with gold, which is reflective, seems to enhance the visibility of defects. Even with all of the careful inspecting and the purchasing of quality blanks, one can still find defects in the final products that can be related to the purchased blanks. And, yes, these defects did affect the value of the item in the consumers' eyes. Today, they affect the value of collected items.

Gold Encrusted Decorating

We begin looking at the decorating of china and glassware by reviewing the steps necessary to apply gold decorations. One thing to remember is that gold applied to an etched surface is thought to have better adhesion than gold applied to an untreated glass or china surface. The etching process made the item rough and thus increased the surface area for adhesion. As an example, many pieces of stemware will have a gold trim line around the top of the rim on an unetched area. Below that is a raised etched gold-decorated pattern. Many times the gold on the rim is badly deteriorated while the etched gold pattern is still in good shape. This result is thought to be at least partly due to the better adhesion of gold to an etched surface.

The first step in preparing a gold decoration on an item (a china plate for example) is to make a detailed drawing of the pattern that one wishes to have on the plate. Of course, the idea for the design had to come first. It is not just the artwork that is important. It is knowing where the desired pattern will be laid out on the plate. Let us assume that our plate is 10" in diameter on the outside edge and we want to make a 1" wide repeating floral design around the outermost part of the plate. For a perfectly circular flat-rimmed plate, we would have to draw two circles on a sketch sheet. The first would have a 5" radius (10" diameter) from the center point, and the second circle, using the same center point, would have a 4" radius (8" diameter). Thus, we have outlined the area within which we must work if this 10" plate is going to have a 1" band around the outside. Usually, the artist would only work with ⅓ (or ¼) of this laid-out area and would make sure that each ⅓ section would match up with every other ⅓ section. The two main reasons for doing this are: 1) the effort to make the design has been cut to ⅓, and 2) laying down three ⅓ sections was much easier to do and much easier to handle than trying to lay down a complete circular rim.

Next, the design artist would fill in the repeating flower pattern around the ⅓ rim on the sketch sheet. Not only are very good artistic skills required if this is to be a product of great beauty, but the artist must have an immediate sense of proportions and know how to lay out the exact number of flowers needed for the ⅓ sections to match up. This also meant that the artist had to be able to convert the sketch to a different diameter plate, hopefully without having to redo the original creative sketch. Many times the sketch would have lines going out from the center to help in establishing the proper proportions for the design. These lines would not be put onto the finished product. While the creatively-sketched design does not have to be absolutely perfect, the better the design, the easier it is to transfer onto the steel plate that will have the etched pattern.

With the design in hand, the artist was now ready to prepare the etch plate. At WDCO, all of this design and steel plate-etch work was done by Karl Knoblich (at location 4E). At other decorating firms, an artist might prepare the sketch and someone else would transfer the design to the steel plate. The eight-pound steel plates were ⅛" thick and 14" by 16" on the sides. To move from the design drawing to the final etched product, a steel plate was first coated with a layer of hot waxy ink. This waxy ink was one of Karl's own secret formulas. This wax was allowed to cool and dry. Then, with magnifying glass in hand, the sketched pattern was scratched into the surface of the wax, exposing the metal below. A variety of different sized scribing tools was used for this process. It was in this one act, the act of scribing a well-designed pattern into the wax on the steel plate, that set the tenor for all of the products that WDCO produced. It was Karl Knoblich who made the difference between a fair product and a really great product. Albert Knoblich remembers his father saying that he (Karl) could engrave a better 20-dollar bill than the government.

After the plate had been scribed and any mistakes corrected (by adding waxy ink to a faulty area and rescribing), the steel plate was ready to be etched. To do this, a dam was built around the area where the design had been scribed. This dam was constructed of wax-coated cardboard and this cardboard was sealed to the steel plate with more molten wax. Strips of cardboard, about 1" high, were cut from stock sheets. A strip would be curved around a portion of the scribed design and warm wax poured along the bottom edge of the cardboard to hold it in place. This process was continued until the entire design was enclosed by the cardboard and wax barrier or dam. Next, nitric acid was poured inside the dam so that it

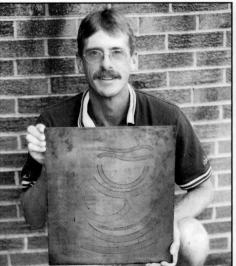

Figure 7. Left: Douglas Norman holding an etched steel plate. The pattern on the plate is Design 33. It is named "Stacked Circles with Inside Diamonds." The steel plate was in a flood and damaged. It weighs eight pounds and is ⅛" x 16" x 14". Doug is the grandson of J. Leland Taylor, next to the last president of WDCO. **Figure 8.** Right: Reverse side of steel plate featuring "Rider and Fox Hunt," showing Design 657. This photograph shows only ¼ of the designs on the back of this plate.

covered the entire design area. This nitric acid then began eating away the exposed metal where the waxy ink coating had been removed. A brush was used to remove air bubbles down in the scribed lines so the steel plate would be uniformly etched. After about an hour, the residual acid was poured off of the steel plate. The cardboard/wax dam was removed and the entire plate was washed with hot water to remove all of the waxy ink and any wax from the cardboard dam. The etched plate was then dried, and it was ready for use. For a large design, it usually took a week to prepare an etched pattern but the preparation was a come-and-go process as Mr. Knoblich had lots of other duties to perform. It should be noted that there could be as many as 15 or 20 different etched designs on a steel plate. It depended on the size of the designs. Importantly, it was this etched-plate process that led to the WDCO becoming a major gold decorator in 1911. Figure 7 shows Lee Taylor's grandson, Douglas Norman, holding an engraving plate given him by Albert Knoblich.

The front of this flood-damaged plate has several engravings of design pattern D-33. This pattern is called "Stacked Circles with Inside Diamonds" and can be seen in more detail in Plate 184 in Chapter 5. Note how the engravings seen on the steel plate Doug is holding in Figure 7 are shaped to fit various sizes and designs of different styles of china or glassware. The back of the steel plate is also engraved and includes an airplane, university mottoes, seals and emblems, fruit, birds, cattails, and a fox hunt scene. A close-up of a portion of the back of this engraving plate is shown in Figure 8. One can see cattails, fruit, and the pattern of the "Rider and Fox Hunt." It is easy to see the water damage on this close-up. Etching plates have to be near pristine in smoothness to be used effectively. In the lower right-hand corner of this photograph, there is etching, ¼" *from bottom*. Then right behind the rider in the Fox Hunt scene is the inscribed instruction, 2" *from the top of the shaker*. The shaker, with this hunt scene and the 2" margin, can be viewed in Plate 482 in Chapter 5 as design D-657. Obviously, when this etched pattern was transferred to the shaker, the engraved instructions were cut away and not included. Also, once transferred, the engraving was decorated with enamel to give the bright vivid colors. The glasses in Plate 483 show another similar hunt scene, but with two riders. Even though both of these designs came from an etch plate (called that because the plate was made by etching the metal) there probably was no acid etching of the glass shaker itself. An image was picked up from the etch plate, transferred to the glass surface, fired (sealed) in a low temperature glass kiln (often pronounced "kill" by the workers), and then returned to an artist for the free-hand painting over the lined design. We will go into this in a little more detail later in this chapter.

Once Karl Knoblich had finished etching a design into a steel plate, just how was the design transferred to the china plate blank? This was done in the Pattern department (3N, 3O, 3P, & 3Q), and the individual at WDCO who coordinated this work and directly handled the etched steel plates was Elmer Shire. He worked in an area called the printing table (3P). When a particular design was called for in decorating a plate, Elmer would go out to the storage bins and retrieve the necessary etched plate. He would take it to his work area and warm the steel

Figure 9. Pulling transfer design from etched and inked steel plate. Photograph shows Elmer Shire. Blackened glove is used as the plate is hot.

plate with a small heater. Shire would then use a putty knife to apply a thick ink/wax mixture to the warmed plate. He would force the mixture down into the entire etched pattern on the steel plate. After all of the etched pattern was filled with the ink/wax mixture, Elmer would use the putty knife to remove the excess from the flat surface of the steel plate. Any excess amounts of this wax left on the surface had to be removed so that the only ink/wax remaining would be in the etched grooves. To get the last traces off the surface, three different cloth-coated hard rollers, each of a different texture, were rolled over the flat plate surface. The texture of these rolling pin-like rollers had to be such that none of the ink/wax was removed from the etched grooves of the design pattern. After a final inspection of the steel plate, the design from the etched grooves was ready to be picked up and transferred to the china blank.

The transfer process was started by cutting a piece of special tissue paper to the size needed to cover the ink/wax pattern on the steel plate. This tissue was placed over the design on the still warm plate and a soft rubber roller was used to press the tissue paper gently down into the ink/wax in the etched grooves. The tissue would pick up this pattern and then the tissue would be gently lifted from the steel plate as seen in Figure 9. The ink/wax mixture would dry almost immediately as it was removed from the warm plate. Because of the depth of the etched pattern and the softness of the rubber roller, this transfer process to the tissue could be repeated three times before the steel plate had to be re-inked.

The character of the ink/wax pattern was very vivid when the tissue paper was turned over with the ink side up. Since the pattern had been turned over, the detail of the design was reversed as far as left to right was con-

Figure 10. This is a negative from pattern Design 75, "Three Birds on Hanging Vine." The negative shows where to trim the transfer tissue for proper placement on a piece of stemware shown to the left. Note the curved lines on the top and left and right sides. These match the curves and rim of the stem and give a uniform layout.

cerned. An easy example of this can be seen by reading a newspaper headline in a mirror. What you get is a reverse of any lettering and it is hard to read unless, of course, you are a typesetter or printer and are familiar with reading backward letters and numbers. The ink/wax mixture on the tissue was well absorbed and did not rub off easily. Karl Knoblich included a few of these ink patterns directly in his design book. Many times the steel plates had patterns that were cut in both directions so the pattern could be used on top of a glass surface or below it, and it would look the same when viewed from above.

Once the design image was on the tissue paper, it was passed to the "pattern girls" to make the transfer to the blank china or glass items. They did their work at a large table called the pattern table (3Q). Elmer Shire would bring the tissue paper with the designs on it to the pattern table. The "pattern girls" would then use small, sharp knives and scissors to help make the design fit perfectly to the surface of the china or glass object being decorated. With complicated items such as a spherical sugar bowl, it was necessary for the ink/wax coated tissue to be made so that it could be folded, cut, or otherwise fitted onto the blank. Since the final etched pattern on the blank needed to appear seamless, the proper shape of the initial etched-plate pattern was very important. It took great skill for these technicians to make the proper adjustments to fit the pattern on irregular shaped items, even under handles on tea cups and sugar bowls. Figure 10 shows a negative of a pattern out of the design book and a glass beside it. This negative shows where the excess tissue should be cut away so that the design would be more easily placed on and around the blank glass or stem. The top of the pattern is curved so it will fit neatly around the top of the stemware without making the pattern curl. Still, as we have studied this process and looked at some very complicated patterns, we are unclear on just how the cut

tissue sheets were made to fit as perfectly as they did.

Once a piece of the tissue paper was in its proper position on a blank, a cloth with an unknown oil on it was rubbed over the tissue surface to help release the ink/wax onto the surface of the glass or china. Because of its smell, the "pattern girls" always thought that the release oil was some form of banana oil. A small brush was often used to assist in getting the banana oil into tight spots on the blank item. The tissue paper was slowly lifted off with the ink/wax pattern being left on the blank. The places on the blank where the ink/wax pattern was laid down were protected and would not be affected by the future hydrofluoric acid etching. For any uncoated areas, the glass or china would be slowly eaten away (etched) by the acid. But before this treatment, the patterned blanks were taken to the "upstairs girl" (next flight up) at the touch-up table (4O). By free-hand, she would add more ink/wax to any problem area an item had. She would repair any cracks or other blemishes in the ink/wax pattern before the item was passed on for the etching process. Thus, she acted as the second quality control inspector for each item, the first having been the inspector of the blanks when they arrived at WDCO.

Before the pattern-containing item was passed on to the next step of the process, the "upstairs girl" probably placed a thin but accurate band of black wax next to the decoration pattern that was on the item. In the next sequence of the process, any part of the decorated item that was not to be affected by the etch solution had to be totally covered with wax. For example, if a sugar bowl was to have an unetched inside and a clear base, it was necessary to coat these areas with wax to protect them from the acid. Thus, the accurate band of wax that the "upstairs girl" put on the item protected the pattern. If some of the later-applied bulk wax got onto the band she had applied, it would not be on the pattern to be etched. It was in the wax room (4Q) that this bulk protective wax was added to the large areas on the blank item which were not to be etched. The molten wax had lampblack in it so it would be easy to tell if some spot on the item were missed and had not been coated with the wax. This wax/lampblack mixture was often called "resist" since it resisted the attack of acid that was reacting and removing portions of the china or glass surface. Karl Knoblich's brother, Max Knoblich, worked in the wax/etching room. After Max had finished his wax coating work, the items to be etched were placed in a tray. Since different pieces required different etch times, (as specified by Karl Knoblich) items were usually done in batches. The depth of the etch on the piece was controlled by the concentration of the acid solution and by how long the item was left in the acid bath. The hydrofluoric acid (called HF) etch bath was located in a separate area behind the wax room and up against the back wall (still in the 4Q area). It had a separate door opening into the wax room. Albert Knoblich said he was only in the HF room once or twice as his father felt it was not a safe place to be. This seems to have been borne out in that when we discussed Max's work with his son, John, he said his father had died of lung problems. There was a ventilating blower in a tall wooden tower above the acid room. By using a pulley, it was possible to position the blower at the top or at the bottom of the tower. It seems that even in those days there were OSHA-type problems. The fire inspector thought that the proper position of the blower was at the top and the insurance inspector felt it should be at the bottom. Thus, the reason for the pulley and the moveable blower; one just had to know which inspector was coming and when.

After the wax was applied to the item, it and other similar items were placed in a rubber-lined metal basket and immersed in the HF solution. Camel hair brushes were again used to make sure there were no air bubbles on the surface to be etched. HF solutions can give very nasty burns, so care had to be taken during this operation not to get any of the acid on one's skin. Long rubber gloves, a rubber apron, and rubber boots were usually worn to protect the worker. Today, a face shield would also be used. Whenever there was a small burn, potash was said to have been rubbed into the affected area.

After the items had been in the acid bath for the required time (usually from 10 to 60 minutes), the etch basket was raised and the acid was allowed to drain back into the vat. After draining, the items were washed in water to remove any residual acid. Then the item went back into the wax room and a hot water bath

was used to remove the wax. The floating wax was skimmed off and returned to the wax pot for reuse. Then there was one more washing of the items before they were set aside for drying, and before being sent to the decorating area. This was the area along the south and west facing windows of the fourth floor.

In the decorating area, the etched and dried items were ready for detailed enhancement. For a gold encrusted item, it was necessary to apply a very fine dispersion of gold. When an entire item was coated with gold, it was called all-over-gold (AOG). Still, that did not mean the inside surface or the underneath portion of the object would necessarily be gold coated. The gold was usually applied to the outside visible etched surfaces. Many times the inside surface of a creamer would be covered with gold while a lidded sugar bowl of the same set would be uncoated on the inside. After an item had been coated with the gold paint, it was set aside to dry. When dry, it was placed in a fairly large, two-handled box. When the box was filled, it was carried to the Kiln Room (4G, 4J, & 4M) where the men would take it and fire the individual items. While gold accounted for almost all of all-over coatings, on a few rare occasions, platinum or palladium dispersions were used to give a sturdy silver look (see Plate 146). To get a good perspective of the overall gold coating process, the author suggests that one stop here and read the article by a teenager in Appendix D.

Karl Knoblich kept the formulas for the gold dispersions his personal secret. He knew how much trouble other companies were having in trying to get very detailed reproductions of their etched and gold decorated patterns onto their blanks. (See Bibliography, Reference 3, pages 32 and 35). Detail and perfection seemed to be personal trademarks of Karl Knoblich. It is known that Karl initially started making his gold dispersions using solid bars of gold bought from the U.S. government. He probably used a very strong acid called aqua regia to dissolve (put into solution) the gold. Aqua regia

Figure 11. Left: Bottle in which powdered gold was shipped. Bottle is 4.4" high and 1.9" in diameter. Bottle has no label but came from Hanovia Chemical and Mfg. Co. of Newark, New Jersey. Gold residue is still in the bottle. **Figure 12.** Right: Wooden box for shipping powdered gold. The gold was purchased from the Hanovia Chemical and Mfg. Co., Newark, New Jersey. The box shows a large swan and is wax sealed to make it tamper resistant. Wax has been spilled over the front of the box.

is one part concentrated nitric acid and three to four parts of concentrated hydrochloric acid. This acid mixture gets its name from the fact that it dissolves the metals of royalty — gold and platinum. Albert remembers seeing ball mills (lidded crocks that contained either metal or ceramic balls) that were continually being rotated to help break up the gold and put it into solution. Once the gold was dissolved, it was brought back out of solution (possibly by dilution with water) so that it would be in the form of very fine gold particles. These particles were then suspended in some liquid or paste so that the gold particles could be painted onto the etched area of a blank. Again, this is mostly speculation as Karl kept his techniques and formulas secret. He had several formulas for dull gold paint and several for bright gold paint. It is known that at some point powdered gold was purchased directly from Hanovia Chemical & Mfg. Co., of Newark, New Jersey. Albert has a glass bottle from this firm that contains 100 grams of "Quid Bright Gold." Figure 11 shows an unlabeled bottle that was used for shipping gold. Several of these bottles were placed in a wooden box for shipping. Figure 12 shows a picture of one of these boxes. The corners of the box were stamped with wax seals to make sure no one tampered with the

Figure 13. Mixing can supposedly be used for gold painting touch-ups. Gold can be seen in the top ⅓ of the can. This part of the can acts as a lid for the bottom section. The lower ⅔ of the can still contains an unknown mixing liquid.

box after it left the manufacturer.

There was one other gold related item that came from WDCO. Figure 13 shows a small can with an

Figure 14. Lee Taylor examining a small vase to be fired in the chinaware kiln beside him. Note the three different sizes of kilns in the room.

unreadable label is shown divided into two parts. The top ⅓ of the can stores gold particles. This gold powder can be seen in the top of the can in the photograph. The bottom ⅔ of the can contains a liquid. The top of the can with the dry powder actually acts as a lid or stopper for the bottom part of the can with the liquid. Was the liquid in the bottom of the can used to disperse the gold from the top? Was this some sort of a touch-up can where you could dip a brush into the liquid and then into the gold? That way one might be able to add a little gold powder to a pattern defect just before the item was kiln fired. The can has not been opened in years so the liquid remains unknown.

When the gold encrusted items were delivered to the Kiln Room, the items were dry to the touch (the gold dispersion liquid had mostly evaporated). The kiln men would take the items and stack them in the kilns. Figure 14 shows items inside a kiln before heating. These photographs were taken in 1952 and were used in an article by the local natural gas company of the Columbia Gas System. In the article, the gas company called these controlled atmosphere, refractory muffle, batch-type kilns. They said the units were fired at temperatures ranging from 1400 to 1700 degrees Fahrenheit. This temperature range provides a tight bond for the gold and china. Lee Taylor, then the WDCO president, is shown inspecting a vase before placing it in the kiln. It appears there is a firing cone on the first layer, front and center. This cone melts at a very specific temperature and is used to tell when the kiln has reached the proper temperature. By Mr. Taylor's feet are ceramic "stacking blocks" used to make more than one level in the kiln. On the floor, farther to his right are fluted "riser blocks" used to hold the stacking blocks. There are three different sizes of kilns in this photograph: the small one to the right, the medium sized one in front of Lee Taylor, and finally, the really big kiln behind him. Notice the box on the floor in front of the large kiln. This was used to stand on so the operator could reach far into the kiln to stack pieces of china. Many times the kiln operator had to crawl into the back of the kiln to properly fill it. WDCO probably had 20 to 25 kilns in the furnace room. The blank of the vase that Lee is holding was made by the Hall China Company (its 641 design), and the vase can be seen in Plate 63. The furnace conditions described by the gas company were those used for firing china or pottery. Later, we will discuss glassware, which has to be fired at much lower temperatures.

When the gold decorated china and pottery items were removed from the kiln they were moved to the polishing area. At the polishing table, the gold was buffed to a brighter luster. Figure 15, with a group of people from

Figure 15. Various WDCO employees gathered around the polishing table in about 1946. Standing left to right are Bill Neibur, an unknown individual, Madelyn Herbrank, and Oliver Crumley. Seated left to right are Hilda Schafer, Walter Rupel, and Irene Tomlinson (Crumley-Dodd).

several areas, shows the polishing table. Note the gold coated burnished items around the table. There were two techniques to do this. The first was a fiberglas type pencil. This looked like an eraser pencil where the paper was unwrapped to expose more of the eraser as needed. The fiberglas pencil was also unwrapped as the contained fiberglas surface was worn down as it polished the gold. This worked fairly well for small areas but for larger pieces, a very fine, wet "sea-sand" was used on a damp rag to do the burnishing or polishing. If all went well and there were no further steps to be added to the decoration, the item was inspected one last time and then wiped clean and sent out for packing. There were no further washings of the items. While we have described this more or less as a "once through process," in actual practice that was not necessarily how it was done. Many times the etched or stamped WDCO logo was fired separately from the decorating step. And if any inspection step found a defect, this defect was corrected, if possible, and then refired. And at times, more than one coat of gold paint was deliberately applied to the item.

This brings us to the interesting point of gold recovery. Bins were located beside the kilns and at other locations so that any imperfect pieces could have the gold recovered from them. Importantly, any rags or other items that were used to clean up spilled gold were also saved for recovery. This recovery was probably done by dissolving the gold, from all these various sources, in aqua regia. The gold would then be recovered from this acid. Today, the rags and damaged items would probably be sent to a recovery company that specializes in this type of work. Within the context of gold recovery, the question always comes up as to the value of the gold on various decorated items, particularly the AOG items. Some people assume that when the gold was put on these items it was probably valued in the range of $35 per ounce. Actually, the price of gold bullion was very constant and from 1900 till 1934, it was valued at $20.67 ounce. Then in 1934, the United States government enacted the Gold Reserve Act at the $35 per ounce rate. This price was still in effect when WDCO closed in 1962. Today, the price of gold is more in the range of $300 per ounce. Should not the old, gold-covered items be worth a great deal today? To help solve this problem, we took two different AOG items (they were broken in shipment to us) and had them analyzed for the amount of gold they contained. This analysis work was done by Ledoux and Company, UCS Section, in Teaneck, New Jersey. Without going into all the details, the analysis showed that the value of the gold was about 5.3¢ per square inch of gold-coated surface, if gold were priced at $300 per troy ounce. Thus, a large all-over-gold celery dish, with 120 square inches of coated surface, would have a gold value of about $6.36. Of course, we, like many others, were hop-

ing that there would be 10 times as much gold on an item as this. Oh, well.

Hand Painted and Enameled Decorating

Many of the gold decorations were put on glass but usually not in an AOG mode. When gold is put on glass it has to be fired at much lower temperatures than those used for china and porcelain items. Gold melts at 1945 degrees Fahrenheit. When put in a furnace or kiln at 1700 degrees Fahrenheit, how does the gold run together if it is below its melting point? It is part of the nature of very small particles that temperature alone does not determine what happens to the particles. "Time at temperature," plays a role in how the particles fuse and join together. Applied pressure could be used to bring about this fusing effect also but there is not a very good or economical technique to do this on china or glass. The "time at temperature" effect can be easily understood when you think of cooking a chicken in an oven for 45 minutes at 400 degrees Fahrenheit. You can get similar results by cooking the chicken for 60 minutes at 350 degrees, or even 300 minutes at 250 degrees. While this is not exactly what happens to gold particles, the "time at temperature" relationship can be envisioned better with this example. Molecular scale interactions help bring about the fusing process for the small gold particles. All this was said in an attempt to help understand why gold particles painted on glass or china can fuse below the melting point of gold. Just as important, it is necessary to realize that glass (and there are lots of varieties of glass) does not have a true melting point but does soften gradually with increasing temperature.

Some glasses soften at temperatures of less than 1000 degrees Fahrenheit. More typical glasses soften at temperatures just under 1300 degrees. The point to make is that glass kilns must be operated at temperatures far below those of china or pottery items. Yet the higher the temperature that can be used, the more rapid the production of wares from that kiln. A 1936 newspaper article (Appendix A) quotes Frank Thurm as saying that the glassware furnaces were fired at 300 degrees and the chinaware furnaces at 1200 degrees. Our guess would be that over the years both of these temperatures were raised to higher levels. With this said we will drop back to the start of the enameling and glassware decorating processes.

The dictionary definition (Webster's dictionary, of course) of enamel reads something like, "A usually opaque vitreous composition applied by heat fusion to the surface of metal, glass, or pottery." A second definition reads, "A usually glossy paint that flows out to a smooth hard coat when applied." Most people are aware of the old enameled pots and pans that had a glossy colored surface. These surfaces were fired onto the "blank" metal items. The same is true for porcelain and glassware. With china-type items, if it was a non-AOG fired design, the piece was often brought to the decorating area (primarily at 4K, 4L, 4N, & 4P). Here a decorator could add enamel highlights to portions of the gold pattern. Sometimes decorators would affix floral or other types of decals to the center of items such as plates. Once these additions had dried at room temperature, the items were usually returned to a lower temperature kiln for the fusing of the enamel or decal with the gold or the china itself.

When design patterns were put on glassware, there were a number of approaches that could be followed. Sometimes the glassware was only etched. Sometimes it was etched and gold coated over the etching. Sometimes it was etched, gold coated over the etching, and then had enamel paint added to highlight other design features. And at other times, a colored background was added to the underside of a glass item to make the design more visible. Black, blue, cobalt, and orange were often used as background paints. Albert Knoblich said that his dad used a secret formula to make the cobalt enamel and that he prepared it in the basement of their home. From a collector's point of view, scratches in these background paints are some of the most frequent faults found in these types of pieces.

In the mid- to late 1930s, WDCO moved toward more and more less formal, decorated items. As noted in Chapter 2, this included items decorated with themes such as sports activities, wildlife, bright geometric designs, boats, horses, and others. While Wheeling kept its traditional lines and AOG items, the company was also following the demands of the marketplace. It began selling commemorative church plates, various items depicting organizational celebrations, and historical recognition ware. Bar ware items became big sellers. Blank pieces of glassware became important starting points. Instead of picking up an etching pattern from a steel plate, the grooves in plates were probably filled with an enamel paint. We assume the enamel paint was picked up by an absorbent tissue paper and then transferred to the surface of the glass item. We have no idea what was used to release the paint from the paper. Nor do we know for certain if the transferred pattern dried at room temperature or if it were kiln dried and fused. We assume the latter is correct. When the ink was dried, the artist/decorators took the items and applied the necessary colored enamels to bring out the uniqueness of the item. Later on, transfer patterns would replace all of this, and the art of hand decorating would almost totally disappear as a commercial process. Figure 16 shows three decorators and one technician working at a decorating table (4K). The unnamed lady technician in the right-hand corner is adding the gold stripes around the rims of the painted glasses. Sometimes she would also add gold paint to the edge of the base of the glass. Since her work is the last step in the glass decorating process, there is a wooden box sitting beside her that she fills before it is taken to the kiln room for the final firing. In front of her on the table are two labeled and corked bottles that say "Hanovia," the source of the gold she is using in her paint. The decorator seated beside her is Frank Richter. He is hand painting what appears to be pattern D-657, "Rider and Fox Hunt," shown in Plate 482. The unknown lady across from him is working on pattern D-486, "Game Birds," shown starting with Plate 378. The decorator beside her is Walter Rupel who was also the vice president of WDCO when this picture was taken in 1952. He is applying enamel paint to some portion of a very wide gold band on a plate. All of the glassware items sitting on the table in the photograph have some form of pre-outlining on them. While the artist has some freedom in colors and technique, there is still a consistency to the final product. We've always wondered if the brown paper bag sitting on top of the florescent light is somebody's lunch, maybe soup, which they are trying to keep warm. Figure 17 is a casual picture of another decorating table. Lidded candy jars can be seen in the upper right corner of this photo. Figure 18 shows Vincent Beck working on his specialty, "Raised Birds," D-622. Plate 434 starts the display series of these birds. Vincent was in his seventies when this picture was taken. It appears that he is laying down a foundation of thick white paint. The way we understand the process, each time, after a layer of paint was laid down on the glass, it was refired. When looking at one of Beck's raised birds it is evident that he is as much a sculptor as he is a painter. It was only with the last coat of enamel that Mr. Beck finally applied the colored enamel. We assume that the completed pieces in the foreground had already had their final firing and were placed in the picture for effect. We doubt that Vincent would paint the gold rims on the items.

Figure 19 shows a glass kiln being loaded for firing by Bill Niebur. The lower firing temperature of the glass kiln allows a sliding tray to be used in place of the ceramic stacking blocks that were shown in the porcelain kiln. The tray at the very bottom of the furnace is probably a baffle to help minimize hot spots in the kiln. We understand there were six glass kilns that were used at WDCO. The expected firing temperature of the kilns must be close to the softening point of the type glass being used. There are at least nine pieces of stemware on the tray he is pushing inward and one can see some sort of white rein-

Figure 16. Wheeling craftspeople decorating china and glassware. Only the two men are identified, Walter Rupel on the left and Frank Richter on the right.

Figure 17. Artists/decorators at a work table in about 1946. Left to right are Herman Schwensen, Frank Richter, Vincent Beck, and an unidentified individual.

forcing that has been wrapped around each stem. Stemware, since it is somewhat top heavy, is known as a bad actor. I have several pieces of stemware (not WDCO) that sag a little to one side. The wrapping must have been a technique they developed to get around this potential problem. The photograph shows what appears to be one white painted glass at the very front of the kiln. This was probably one of Vincent Beck's base coats that was being fired, and the glass was being prepared for the next coat of enamel in his "Raised Birds" series.

There are a couple of other processing and production details of WDCO to be recognized. In the mid-1940s, a move was made away from the use of steel etching plates towards a stone lithographic process. Lithography is a process that depends on the mutual repulsion of water and grease. If a waxy grease drawing is made on a very flat slab of limestone, then the waxy grease area will preferentially attract an oily ink when the stone surface is damp. The water on the stone repels the ink and the waxy grease attracts it. This entire process is thus carried out on a smooth stone on which the printing area (waxy grease) is no higher than the non-printing area (water). If an inked roller were passed over a lithographed stone, the ink would go to the waxy grease area and none of the ink would be left on the dampened water area of the stone. Then, if a piece of paper (like the tissue paper in the steel etch plate process) were placed on the stone, it would pick up the ink from the waxy grease. The image on the paper then could be transferred to a piece of china or glassware. Importantly, the waxy grease outline remains on the lithographic stone and can be used over and over for more inkings. Since WDCO already had the images on the steel etch plates, most likely there wasn't much the artists had to do to convert their patterns to the lithographic stones. It may have been as easy as filling the grooves in the etch plate with the proper type of waxy grease, then lifting this pattern as they had before, and transferring it directly to the stone surface. Then, the lithography stone was ready for use as a much simpler process for transferring patterns to blanks to be decorated. Whether photoengraving was ever a part of WDCO technology is unclear. We have heard that there was experimentation with some of the early silkscreen techniques. We have no physical evidence of this though. There are a couple of unnumbered drawings in the Design book which could be silkscreen patterns. We do know that they experimented with different types of engraving processes.

Figure 20 is a picture of Albert Knoblich holding an experimental copper plate that was etched

Figure 18. Vincent Beck producing "Raised Birds."

Figure 19. Bill Niebur loading a glass kiln. Notice the supports on the stemware.

Figure 20. Albert Knoblich's surprise — an etched copper plate.

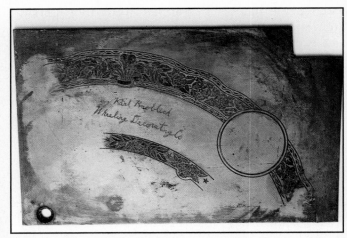

Figure 21. Close-up of etched copper plate. Plate is approximately 6½" long, 4" wide, and ³⁄₁₆" thick.

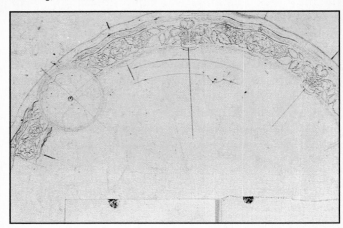

Figure 22. Copper plate pattern from WDCO Design book. The pattern was loose in the Design book and is unnumbered.

with the close-up pattern shown in Figure 21. He has no idea why this test was made, or even the significance of the test. Parts of the design pattern for this test are found in two separate locations in the WDCO Design book, but both are unnumbered patterns. A very faint copy of one of these is shown in Figure 22.

The Design book also shows a pattern that was outlined by a series of very small pinholes. These pinholes are representative of a technique called "pouncing." During the pouncing process, the artist would first create a design or pattern on a piece of lightweight paper. Then, when the design was finished, small holes were pricked into the lines of the entire pattern. Then the transfer paper design was laid over a blank such as a plate. The design would be centered on the plate and carbon black or some other compound would be sprinkled over the design. Usually, a cloth bag filled with sand was tapped (pounced) over the now carbon-coated design pattern. A gentle pouncing action would force the carbon through the pattern where the pinholes were located and onto the underlying plate. After this had been done over the entire pattern, the piece of tracing paper was lifted and a portrayal of the design was left on the plate. The end result was similar to transferring an inked image from a metal etch plate to a blank. In both cases the decorator was free to show artistic expression, but within the confinement of the dotted or otherwise transferred pattern placed upon

the blank ware. While carbon was usually used with a pounce bag, the items in the WDCO Design book indicate that they may have used some finely ground reddish colored material. It looks like a red ocher colored powdered pumice.

Time and research will uncover more of the details about how the various operations of the WDCO were performed. It is the need to find the correct resources and the correct people so the best available information about these techniques can be historically preserved. We conclude this chapter by including a list of people who worked at WDCO. We assume there are several misspellings, transposed maiden and married names, and names that we just failed to uncover. Again, we hope that we can improve this list in the future.

Employees of the Wheeling Decorating Company

Name	Role/Work Area	Name	Role/Work Area
Vincent Beck	Decorator	Bill Niebur	Kiln Area
James Briggs	Kiln Area	Betty Nickols	Decorator
Frank Bishop	China Packer	Hilda Nickols	Decorator
Helen Bober	Upstairs Girl, Touch-Up	Helen Olako	Print Room
Josephine Bober	Touch-Up Girl	Richard Otto	Head Salesman
Eliza Bole	Decorator	Mrs. _____ Pearl	Packaging
Martha Bruhn	Decorator	Arley Postlewait	Pattern Department
Elizabeth Buczek	Decorator	Mr. _____ Porter	Glass Cutting Machine
Pat Conroy	Decorator	Louise Rice	Decorator
Oliver Crumley	Office Manager, then President	Frank Richter	Decorator
		Ethel Riley	Decorator
Ginney Dailer	Decorator	Mary Riley	?
Frank Decker	Packer-Shipper	Joseph Roi	Print Room
Robert Engelhardt	Part owner - Decorator	Walter Rupel	Decorator, then Vice President
Virginia Gates	Decorator		
Marquite Greer	Decorator	Hilda Schafer	?
Madelyn Hebrank	Decorator	Genevieve Schmalstieg	Pattern Department
Bertha Heyman	Washing Room	Helen Schneider	Pattern Department
Josephine Hurdzan	Decorator	Herman Schwensen	Decorator
Mrs. _____ Jones	Polishing Table	Elmer Shire	Printing Table and Pattern Supervisor
Karl Knoblich	Production Supervisor, Designer	Helen Snyder	Decorator
Max Knoblich	Wax Room, Etching Vat	Ann Tappe	Touch-Up-Girl
May Landmeyer	Decorator	Lee Taylor	Head Salesman, then President
Howard Lash	Decorator		
Nellie Martin	Polishing Table	Frank Thurm	Owner
Mildred Mazelon	Print Table	Mrs. _____ Tilford	Wax Room Clean-Up
Mr. _____ Miller	Decorator	Irene Tomlinson-Crumley-Dodd	Decorator
Mary Milonovich	Print Room	Ann Vogler	Pattern Department
Mildred Milonovich	Decorator	Gertrude Vogler	Pattern Department
Helen Mooney	Decorator	Virginia Vogler	Pattern Department
Olive Muegge	Pattern Department	James Warren	Kiln Area
Mildred Mumley	?	Margaret Weir	Polishing Table
Ceil Munas	Pattern Department	Emma Welchley	Pattern Department
Lucille Munas	Decorator	Ruth West	Decorator
Mildred Munas	Pattern Department	Joseph Yeager	Stock Room - Shipping
Nick Myers	Printing Table, Pattern Supervisor	_____ Zimmerman	Decorator

A source for information on the marks, trademarks, and logos used by WDCO is almost nonexistent. Only two are shown in the WDCO Design book, and these are patterns (TM-G and TM-H) used to put etched logos on the bottom of decorated items. About the only information we could find was in *Lehner's Encyclopedia of U. S. Marks*. (See Bibliography, page 516 of Reference 5) Two of the Wheeling marks are shown in that encyclopedia, along with a very short description of the history of WDCO. As we began collecting, we rapidly found that there were several more than the two from the encyclopedia. The trademarks found to date are shown in the accompanying photographs taken directly from the bottom of decorated items. Throughout the text of this book the trademarks are listed as TM's, starting with TM-C, going through TM-O. Some will question why we skipped TM-A and TM-B. In Chapter 2, we spoke of Albert Knoblich, remembering he once saw a plate in an antique shop with a TM of "Frank Thurm China Co., Whg. W. VA." It is in anticipation of finding this, and maybe another early TM, that we have skipped TM-A and TM-B.

Marks TM-C and TM-D were first found by Douglas Norman as he searched antique shops for new and interesting WDCO items. He purchased three sets of cups and saucers, each with a beautiful design (D-34) which we choose to call "Anhingas and Urns." An anhinga is a large water bird. This design is shown in Plate 186. Two D-33 borders surround the D-34 design and the border is called "Stacked Ovals with Inside Diamonds" (Plate 184). Each of these cup and saucer blanks had a trademark that showed they had been made by Schkacken-Werth Antoinettel. On two of the blanks, the trademarks had been covered over with gold. On two more, the manufacturers' trademarks were still present but the "THURM" trademark (TM-C) had been added. On the final two blanks, gold again obliterated the Antoinettel trademark but this was over-stamped with the design of "TM-D." Since the design D-34 probably was not used before the 1913 time period, one would guess that this was a test program to see how these two trademarks held up in use and public acceptance.

Recently, we found another item with the TM-C trademark. Douglas Norman also purchased a WDCO soup bowl (with the D-2a design pattern) from the Internet which also shows the TM-D logo. Since we know that the business was in some form of operation as early as 1900, we have assumed that there are earlier trademarks yet to be found. While we can certainly understand that TM-C and TM-D might be the earliest marks, we have some reservations. The scrolled "WHEELING DEC. CO., W.VA." found on TM-E and TM-F could have been used by WDCO right from the start of the business.

In listing these trademarks, we have shown both

red and green versions. The intensity and shading of these colors do vary some. Certainly, the gold over the marking of a foreign blank manufacturer's name and country was something that was widely used before about 1917. The U.S. clamped down on this practice, requiring that the country of origin be imprinted on all imported items. Thus, the practice stopped and trademarks like TM-E were no longer acceptable when they covered and obscured importation information.

Before discussing more about the timelines of the various WDCO marks, it is interesting to look at TM-D. Just what is the structure on that logo? Initially, we felt that it was the front of the old suspension bridge, still in Wheeling. This bridge is probably one of the first large suspension bridges in the U.S. Its design even pre-dates the Brooklyn Bridge. It is located only a few blocks

TM-C. This is the hard to read "Thurm" trademark. So far, this logo has been found only on cups and saucers with the D-34 pattern on them. Size: .55" across the tips.

TM-C (2). This is an overmark of the "Thurm" trademark. This provides a better understanding of its appearance.

TM-D. This trademark is called "Fort Henry Near Wheeling." The example shown is over gold which covers the Antoinettel trademark. Size: .52" in diameter.

away from the WDCO plant site. In my own mind I felt that the lines in front of the structure looked a little like suspension cables. Other Wheeling natives have said that the structure is probably Fort Henry which was located close to Wheeling, and that the top of the structure looks like parapet, used to protect soldiers. There is even a flag on top of the structure. A heroic defense at Fort Henry is often called "the last battle of the American Revolution." Bowing to well-placed pressure, we have agreed to call TM-D, "Fort Henry near Wheeling."

It is unclear when the marks TM-G and TM-H were first used. They certainly complicated the manufacturing process in that their pattern had to be first transferred to the blank, just like any other complicated design. Then the trademark had to be etched in the hydrofluoric acid bath and then cleaned and dried.

Then the etched logo was painted with gold and fired in a furnace. Many times this could be done simultaneously with the production of the decorative design on the blank. At other times, because of kiln stacking procedures, it had to be "fired" by itself. Still, it appears that these two trademarks were used before 1925 and were continued until the start of WWII.

When the "cheaper" TM-J came into use is also unclear. TM-J was not etched but stamped onto the decorated blank, using a gold ink. This gold ink dispersion was much thinner than the ones used to do the decorating. Usually, TM-J color appears to be a washed-out red or bluish silver. When viewed at an angle, the mark shows signs of being gold.

The TM-I mark seems to have been with WDCO almost from the start. It was used primarily on small items such as demitasse cups. Our best guess right now is

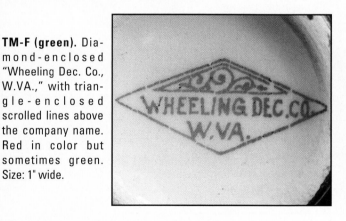

TM-E (red). Diamond-enclosed "Wheeling Dec. Co., W.VA.," with scrolled lines above the company name. All of this is over a gold obscuring oval. Color is usually red but sometimes green. Size: 1" wide.

TM-E (green). Diamond-enclosed "Wheeling Dec. Co., W.VA.," with scrolled lines above the company name. All of this is over a gold obscuring oval. Color is usually red but sometimes green. Size: 1" wide.

TM-F (green). Diamond-enclosed "Wheeling Dec. Co., W.VA.," with triangle-enclosed scrolled lines above the company name. Red in color but sometimes green. Size: 1" wide.

TM-F (red). Diamond-enclosed "Wheeling Dec. Co., W.VA.," with triangle-enclosed scrolled lines above the company name. Red in color but sometimes green. Size: 1" wide.

TM-G. Gold embossed, thin, diamond-shaped, etched mark containing the words, "Wheeling Decorating, W. Co. VA., Glass, China." Size: 1.3" wide.

TM-H. The same as mark TM-G but the enclosing diamond is taller. It is sometimes called a squared diamond. Size: 1.3" wide.

that it was first used in the late teens. We have recently found examples where there is "W.VA." added above or below the mark, but in the same type of printing. It probably depended in part on how much space was available on the item being marked.

At the start of WWII, a gold-colored sticker (TM-K) replaced the etched or stamped marks that had been used. Finding an intact TM-K sticker is difficult to do. Usually just pieces of a sticker are found. Before we found the almost whole one shown as TM-K, we had patched together two pieces of the stickers from different sources. It would have worked for photographing but the diagonal line across it may have looked a little strange. The Hutschenreuther trademark beside the photograph of TM-K presents an interesting question. Was WDCO selling on-hand stock of German china during WWII, or was the sticker still being used in 1945 and 1946 when purchases may have been restarted with Hutschenreuther? Please note that TM-L is often found with the TM-K stick-

er. Though not a trademark, TM-L may be found by itself on WDCO items and thus helps to verify that an item is Wheeling Decorating even though the sticker is missing.

Homer Laughlin made "Eggshell Theme" plates during WWII and into the late 1940s. Maybe there was a good supply of these left over, but we have some of these plates with a manufacturing date as late as 1952. TM-M is the trademark that was used to cover the Homer Laughlin trademark on many of these plates. We don't know why this was done but it could have been a requirement placed on WDCO for the use of these plates. Some of the time (the 1952 plate), the Laughlin mark was not covered over but TM-J was used beside it. Regardless of the reason for it, the TM-M mark has to be one of the worst looking trademarks ever used. In stamp collecting, this would be called a "killer cancel." These Homer Laughlin plates were used by Wheeling for church plates (usually a money making project for the church), bird plates, school plates, animal plates, and so on.

TM-I. Reads "Wheeling Decorating Co.," in block letters. Sometimes has a "W.VA." added above or below the trademark. It is usually seen on smaller items. Size: Varies, with the word "Wheeling" being from .45" to .85" long.

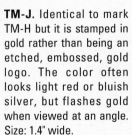

TM-J. Identical to mark TM-H but it is stamped in gold rather than being an etched, embossed, gold logo. The color often looks light red or bluish silver, but flashes gold when viewed at an angle. Size: 1.4" wide.

TM-K. This is a gold colored sticker used by WDCO during WWII. It is shown beside a Hutschenneuther mark. These are hard to find even in fair condition. The inside of the gold oval reads "Wheeling Decorating Co.," with a scripted "W" in a center oval. Often seen with "Decorated in U.S.A." Size: Oval, .6" high and .45" wide.

TM-L. This is not a trademark or a logo. It is simply the block letters "Decorated in U.S.A." It was often used with the TM-K sticker during WWII While not a logo it may help in identifying a WDCO item if a sticker has been removed. Size: The word "Decorated" varies from .45" to .6" long.

TM-M. A black circular over-stamp used to cover the Homer Laughlin, "Eggshell Theme" logo. Only a small "Wheeling Dec. Co." is showing. Was used from WWII to the late 1940s. Size: 1.3" high and 1" wide.

About the time Mr. Thurm died, logo TM-N began appearing. The appearance of this mark may have been the result of incorporation and the new management team. Still, for the first time the "gold" aspects of the business are shown on the trademark. This is a stamped trademark which, again, usually has to be tilted to see the gold reflection of the ink. We suppose that TM-O was introduced about the same time. These last two logos are found frequently but did not seem to get quite as much use as did TM-J.

TM-N. A boxed logo hat reads "Wheeling Gold Chin" with "Wheeling W.VA." under the name and a pair of lines in the box. Color is usually gray to black but flashes gold when viewed at an angle. Size: 1.4" wide and 1" high.

TM-O. Identical to TM-N but the top, bottom, and right-hand side of the box are missing. Still has a double line separating the company name and the city and state. Size: The left line is .8" long and the double line is 1" long.

Chapter 5: Designs, Pictures, and Prices

The design patterns shown in this chapter are some of many listed in the WDCO Design Book. These patterns are the ones we have been able to verify as production items and, so far, this accounts for only about 20 percent of the Wheeling design numbers. In addition, we have found and included in this chapter other designs that are marked with the WDCO logo, backstamp, or trademark, but that are not included in the WDCO Design manual or its numbering system. We know that there was a second Design Book, and most of these items were probably included in that book. The numbering system in the first book stops at item D-328 and on the last few numbers it was written, "new book." We have added more than 100 of our own numbers for these known Wheeling Decorating items and have left room for more numbers. Available pictures, etch plate copies, advertisements, and other written associations were important in the verification work for this additional numbering process. We have skipped the numbers from D-320 to D-599, so if we find D-number information about a design, we can use the original WDCO pattern number. We have already done that with one pattern set showing a large variety of birds. We recently found this set on an etch plate with a D-486 number and the word "Birds" in the middle. All of the WDCO assigned design numbers and our added numbers are given in Chapter 6. As is stated at the start of that chapter, we have also added our own identifying names to all of the patterns. We tried to make the names descriptive as to what the important part of the design was.

An important question to be asked is why have we not gone ahead and shown the other design patterns that are listed in the WDCO Design Book? There are three main reasons for this. First, we do not have a good method of doing this. There are hundreds of designs, or pieces of designs, in the Design Book; too many to just dump into this chapter as random bits of information. Many of these images are of poor quality and this often leads to confusion. Hopefully, these items can be arranged and ordered in a logical sequence. Second, many of the designs probably were never used. A few of these are marked in the design manual simply as "not used." Finally, the Oglebay Museum will have to determine how it wants to make available or disseminate this information to the general public. The Museum is well aware of the potential value these items hold in assisting future research about the Wheeling Decorating Company. Though the quality is not good, there is also a large number of steel plates which were machine copied to make paper duplicates. We will try to keep the general public abreast of new numbers and new WDCO items as we find them or as they are shared with us by others. Contact us through our e-mail address in the front of this book or write to us at home. This will hopefully be one of the main research sources for information about the WDCO. And that is what we hope to provide in this book: links to the past that bring items to the present for current and future enjoyment and understanding.

Confusing WDCO Design Patterns

There are a few WDCO patterns which cause confusion. These are some of the very early designs, and we will try and give a listing of some of the criteria that we think necessary to verify that a particular pattern is truly from WDCO. We say this realizing that we can never be 100 percent sure that an item is not WDCO. Someone could say that a particular plain, gold-banded glass was made by WDCO and we would have no basis for saying it was or was not. Many different decorating companies put simple gold bands on glassware. A classic example of this uncertainty is the gold decoration on the Candlewick pattern from the Imperial Glass Company as shown in Plates 1 and 2. We had a meeting at the Wheeling Library of people who had worked at WDCO. One of the things the workers laughed about was the tedium of painting gold on the small beaded stems on the candlewick items. They talked about painting thousands of these items. Yet today, while we have many of these items in our collection, we cannot know for certain that any particular item was painted by the WDCO crew.

We will talk about four of the WDCO patterns that are most confusing. The confusion comes mainly from the fact that these were designs that were modified only slightly from much earlier designs of other manufacturers. And many companies were implementing these types of designs. They were often used as mirror images so that in one design a part of the design would be pointing to the right and in another design modification, that part would be pointed to the left. It is desirable to have a copy of the known WDCO design on hand to make a good verification. Even then, it is not an easy job. We can never be certain that another etch plate of one of these designs was not made and that it was slightly different from the designs we have at present. The problem becomes even more difficult when trying to make an online purchase of these confusing patterns. In most online photographs, the shown details are not clear enough to make an accurate verification as to the pattern being WDCO. Only 25% of the items we have purchased online, thinking they were one of these difficult designs, have turned out to be correct.

Plates 3 and 4 show mirror images of pattern D-2a. Plate 9 also shows this pattern in clearer detail. These plates were taken directly from the WDCO Design Book. We also have etch plate copies that show this particular pattern in several different sizes. This design is based on a Minton pattern and was used by numerous decorating companies. It is of medium width and is generally used on the rims and edges of various types of glassware. The design is uniform around the pattern and the WDCO design is crisp in its detail.

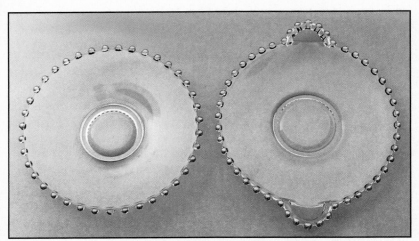

Plate 1. Glass plate; 7h x 7d.; .9h x 8.5l. "Candlewick with Gold Beaded Stems"; Imperial Glass Company. Plain, $20.00 – 35.00; handled, $25.00 – 45.00. WDCO decorated?

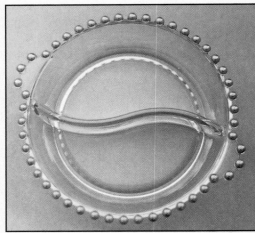

Plate 2. Divided glass dish. 1.3h x 7.1w. "Candlewick with Gold Beaded Stems," Imperial Glass Company. $30.00 – 50.00. WDCO decorated?

Plate 3. D-2a (1). "Fingered Swirls, Arrows, and Flowers." Availability: plentiful. From the WDCO Design Book.

Plate 4. D-2a (2). "Fingered Swirls, Arrows, and Flowers." Availability: plentiful. Mirror image of Plate 3.

There are at least eight necessary details that aid in defining the D-2a pattern:

- In relation to the dotted trim enclosing the pattern, the eight-petal (not six) flower with the dot in the center has one petal at the top and one at the bottom.
- The fingered swirl, going to the arrowhead, has from six to eight distinct fingers, depending on the size of the item to be decorated.
- Again, depending on the size of the item to be decorated, there are from three to five fingers or spikes on the stem right before the flower.
- There is an elongated teardrop (or tapered stick), and a retort shaped curved line on each side of the arrowhead. This long teardrop usually ends about where the stem joins the arrowhead. The space between each of these (the tear drop and the curved line) and the arrowhead is generally uniform and parallel with the arrowhead.
- The well-formed, retort-shaped curve, right before the fingers on the stem going to the flower, has one or two dots by it. The other retort curve by the arrowhead is completely formed and has one dot by it.
- As the stem to the arrowhead leaves the fingers, there is a dimpled box on the stem.
- The top of the arrowhead is narrow, being between ⅓ and ½ as wide as the arrowhead is long.
- Almost touching the fingers on the stem leading to the eight-petal flower is a triangle shape, and this shape has curved sides. Inside this triangle is a closed box with only a narrow line for the side of the box facing the flower.

After rereading the above list, I'm not sure it is worth trying to track this information down. Still, the items are out there as we have many copies from etch plate duplications.

The WDCO design number D-2b is another Minton border pattern that is shown in the Design Book. Mirror images of this pattern are shown in Plates 5 and 6. While I have purchased several items very close in design to this pattern, I have never found an exact match. Thus, there are no decorated items shown or priced for this pattern. We show this pattern to give design information for those who want to conduct the difficult search for this pattern. The general pattern type was used by many others for decorating. The D-2b pattern can be described as being composed of arrowheads, flowers, and a finger-like swirl, which some call a hammer-like projection at the end of one of the leafed swirls. They say that it reminds them of the hammer on the Arm and Hammer Baking Soda box. Whatever the design, these patterns have a boundary of dots on each side acting as a border.

To make an accurate assessment of the D-2b design, it is almost necessary to have the copy from the design manual and a magnifying glass to make a side-by-side comparison. Still, there are six items that are useful in helping to identify a possible D-2b design by WDCO:

- The design is crisp and uniform, not fuzzy.
- There are eight distinct petals on the flower (with a fairly large dot in the center), two on the top edge, two on the bottom, and two on each side.
- On the stem going to the eight-petal flower, there is a wavy, box-like projection and it sometimes touches the swirl to the hammer stem.
- The stem coming backwards from the hammer enlarges as it forms into the arrowhead. It looks almost like the arrowhead could go either direction.
- The sides of the triangle, under the arrowhead, are slightly curved, not straight.
- The loop with the dot, near the tip of the arrowhead, touches or almost touches one of the projections on the hammer swirl.

The design pattern in Plate 7 is not really all that confusing but is shown here because there are other similar

Plate 5. D-2b (1). "Hammer Ending Swirls, Arrows, and Flowers." Scarce availability at best. From the WDCO Design Book.

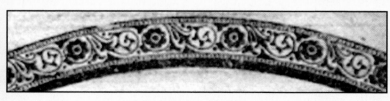

Plate 6. D-2b (2). "Hammer Ending Swirls, Arrows, and Flowers." Scarce availability at best. Mirror image of Plate 5. From the WDCO Design Book.

Plate 7. D-3. "Laurel Leaves with Multiple Dots." Scarce availability. From the WDCO Design Book.

Plate 8. D-10. "Rambler Rose." Scarce availability. From the WDCO Design Book.

WDCO designs and many other decorators who used the laurel leaf-type pattern. The design is a medium width pattern generally used as a trim or in combination with another pattern. The leaves are connected almost head to tail, but are not directly above each other as pairs. The D-3 design shows the connected laurel leaves, with seven to 10 dots behind each leaf. The pattern is contained by two solid lines, with one usually being wider than the other. Importantly, the laurel leaves don't touch the outside solid bands. This multiple dot pattern is also seen in a tracing from an etching plate, but the dots there tend to follow after each other. Within the WDCO Design Book, there are at least three other laurel leaf patterns. Each of these other patterns are borders from other complex designs. Many of the WDCO numbered designs were broken apart and used in other mixed patterns. One of the other laurel patterns is one in which the leaves have a single dot behind them (D-3a), but the leaves do just touch the solid bands, enclosing this part of the total design. The other design (D-3b) is seen as part of D-58 and sometimes as the outside border on D-67. With D-3b, there are four dots behind each leaf, but here again the leaves do not touch the outer solid bands (Plate 22). This design pattern is also seen on tracings from etched metal plates and is the most common of the laurel leaf designs. Still, the laurel pattern is simple enough that we cannot be certain there are not even more D-3 types to be found. And, just because a laurel pattern has four dots behind each leaf does not mean it was made by WDCO.

Plate 8 is the WDCO design of a very common pattern found on many items of decorated glassware. The single record we have for the WDCO design shows a couple of unique details that help to readily identify their design. Again, WDCO could have modified this design later, but we have no other record than what is in the Design Book. This "Rambler Rose" pattern is also contained by solid bands, with one being thicker than the other. Basically, the design is a repeating pattern of three connected roses with hanging leafed vines. All of this is on a background of thin lines connecting the two solid borders. There are three unique parts to this design. At the connecting point where the pattern repeats itself there is a round piece of fruit and a leaf hanging down. These two items are curved towards each other. Most other "Rambler Rose" patterns have two round pieces of fruit hanging down and not a leaf. At the location where the pattern repeats itself and the fruit is hanging down, the background

lines are the longest and most visible and go almost all the way through the design. The center rose is enclosed by four triangle-shaped leaves.

In summary, these are four difficult and confusing patterns. We just don't know if WDCO did any later modifications to these early patterns shown in its Design Book. If we had all of their etched printing plates, then we would know what changes had been made. Modifications were often made when a design had to go onto a different or an unusual shaped blank. Thus, for many of these designs, when they were used as stand-alone borders, it is best to say that the item appears to be WDCO. When there are other WDCO patterns used with these borders, then the results can be clear. In the photographic section coming up, we will show the examples we have for three of these confusing patterns. There will be many items in the rest of this chapter where there is no confusion about which company decorated a particular blank.

As much as possible, we will try to show photographs of design pattern enlargements which have been taken directly from china or glassware items. We will then show various items that have that pattern on them. We use a variety of names to describe the items in the photographs. We do this in part to show the general usage of some of the more common terms. Thus, for example, a flip bowl is used interchangeably with the term "mushroom bowl."

The patterns and photographs will be presented in the numerical order of the design numbers. Thus, we will start with design enlargement D-2a. Later in this chapter, you will find many of the design patterns do not need enlargements. Although there is no pricing information for the enlargements there is availability information as outlined in the Notes and Conventions section on page 6. Values given are for items in very good to excellent condition. Most glassware and porcelain books price only for excellent condition. Decorated items are difficult to find in very good condition, let alone in excellent or pristine condition. Rather than change definitions of these quality categories, we have moved the pricing to cover a little lower quality, but not much lower. One will see very quickly that many of the items we have photographed are not in excellent condition. A few are only fair, at best. Since we had no access to large collections, we were often forced to take what we could find. Still, one should have little trouble in identifying an item as having been decorated by the Wheeling Decorating Company.

Plate 9. Design enlargement; D-2a; "Fingered Swirls, Arrows, and Flowers"; reasonable availability; Minton based design pattern.

Plate 10. Eight-sided dish; 1.2h x 4.7w; D-2a; "Fingered Swirls, Arrows, and Flowers"; no trademark, no blank. $25.00 – 45.00.

Plate 11. Bread plate; 0.6h x 6.2d; D-2a; "Fingered Swirls, Arrows, and Flowers"; no trademark, no blank; Hutschenreuther, Selb L.H.S., Bavaria. $15.00 – 25.00.

Plate 12. Covered candy dish; 3.5h x 6.9d; D-2a; "Fingered Swirls, Arrows, and Flowers"; no trademark, no blank. Heisey. $65.00 – 95.00.

Plate 14. Ten-panel sherbet; 3h x 3.9d; D-2a; "Fingered Swirls, Arrows, and Flowers"; no trademark, no blank. Note: Also has machine cut pattern, assumed to be WDCO. See Plate 15. $35.00 – 55.00.

Plate 13. Irish coffee mug; 5.5h x 2.9d; D-2a; "Fingered Swirls, Arrows, and Flowers"; no trademark, no blank. $45.00 – 65.00.

Plate 15. Close-up of 10-panel sherbet; 3h x 3.9d; D-2a; "Fingered Swirls, Arrows, and Flowers"; no trademark, no blank. Note: A central flower with ferns and individual spear-shaped leaves. This item is machine cut. $35.00 – 55.00.

Plate 16. Unlidded compote or candy jar; 4.7h x 3.5d; D-2a; "Fingered Swirls, Arrows, and Flowers"; no trademark, no blank. $25.00 – 45.00.

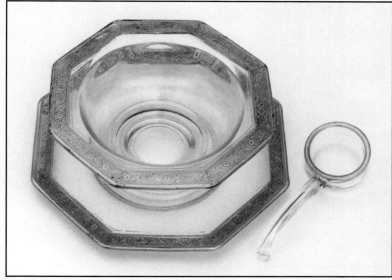

Plate 17. Mayonnaise plate and ladle; 0.7h x 8d; 2.5h x 6.6d; D-2a; "Fingered Swirls, Arrows, and Flowers"; no trademark, no blank. $60.00 – 95.00.

Plate 18. Cruet; 5.2h x 2.5d; D-2a; "Fingered Swirls, Arrows, and Flowers"; no trademark, no blank. $100.00 – 150.00.

Plate 19. Sandwich tray with blue; 5.2h x 11.5d; D-2a; "Fingered Swirls, Arrows, and Flowers"; no trademark, no blank. Note: Light yellow design on the top of the handle. $60.00 – 95.00.

Plate 20. Glass salt shaker; 2.5h x 2.1d; D-2a; "Fingered Swirls, Arrows, and Flowers"; no trademark, no blank. $80.00 – 120.00 for pair.

Plate 21. Soup bowl; 1.8h x 3.2d; D-2a; "Fingered Swirls, Arrows, and Flowers"; TM-D, no blank; Note: Rare trademark. $75.00 – 110.00.

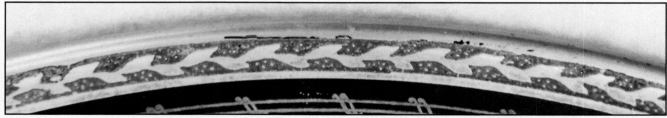

Plate 22. Design enlargement; D-3b; "Laurel Leaves with Four Dots"; infrequent availability. Note: See D-58 an D-67 where D-3b is part of the designs. Plate 7 shows the design pattern for D-3.

Plate 23. Shallow compote; 2.5h x 5.2d; D-3b; "Laurel Leaves with Four Dots"; no trademark, no blank. $20.00 – 35.00.

Plate 24. Small almond dish; 1.4h x 2.9d; D-3b; "Laurel Leaves wit Four Dots"; no trademark, no blank. $20.00 – 35.00.

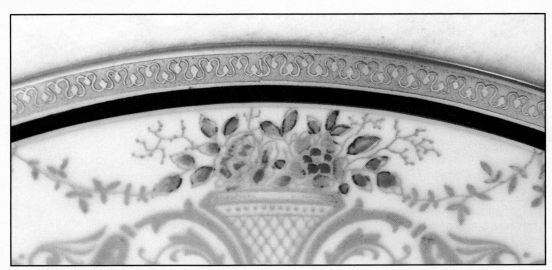

Plate 25. Design enlargement; D-6; "Diamond Connected 'M's' or 'W's'"; rare; Hobart etching. Note: See D-100a for the uses of this border.

Plate 26. Design enlargement; D-7; "Roses and Thorns"; scarce.

Plate 27. Creamer and sugar; 3.4h x 4d, 4.1h x 6d; D-7; "Roses and Thorns"; no trademark, no blank; JHR Hutschenreuther, Selb, Bavaria. $40.00 – 65.00.

Plate 28. Covered butterdish; 3.5h x 6.8d; D-7; "Roses and Thorns"; no trademark, no blank; JHR Hutschenreuther, Selb, Bavaria. $95.00 – 130.00.

Plate 29. Wine glass; 6.6h x 3.1d; D-7; "Roses and Thorns"; no trademark, no blank. $35.00 – 60.00.

Plate 30. Vegetable dish; 1.9h x 10d; D-7; "Roses and Thorns"; no trademark, no blank; Hutschenreuther Selb L.H.S. $40.00 – 65.00. Note: Smaller dish 1.5h x 9.5D, valued at $35.00 – 60.00; dinner plate, $30.00 – 50.00; cup and saucer, $30.00 – 50.00; bread plates or berry bowls, $20.00 – 30.00 each.

Plate 31. Design enlargement; D-10; "Rambler Rose"; infrequent availability. See notes on this item on page 52.

Plate 32. Mayonnaise bowl and plate; dish 3.4h x 7.2d, plate 1.1h x 8.5d; D-10; "Rambler Rose"; no trademark, no blank. $60.00 – 95.00.

Plate 33. Large pink "flip" bowl; 2.1h x 11.3d; D-10; "Rambler Rose"; no trademark, no blank. $35.00 – 75.00.

Plate 34. Short stemmed glass; 4.2h x 3.1d; D-10; "Rambler Rose"; no trademark, no blank. $25.00 – 35.00.

Plate 35. Design enlargement; D-11; "Doves, Roses, and Daisies"; abundant availability. Note: Probably placed in service around 1912.

Plate 36. Small vase; 4.2h x 3.2l x 2w; D-11; "Doves, Roses, and Daisies"; TM-G, blank: 14. $25.00 – 35.00.

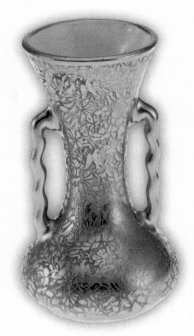

Plate 37. Small vase, 4.7h x 2.6d; D-11; "Doves, Roses, and Daisies"; TM-O, blank: 174. $25.00 – 35.00.

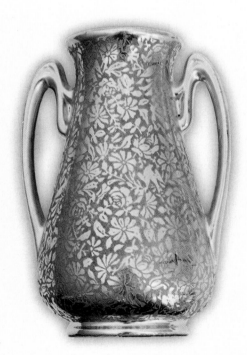

Plate 38. Small handled vase; 4.9h x 2.9d; D-11; "Doves, Roses, and Daisies"; blank: 1049. $25.00 – 40.00.

Plate 39. Eared vase; 4.2h x 3.4d; D-11; "Doves, Roses, and Daisies"; TM-G, blank: 15. $20.00 – 35.00.

Plate 40. Small trophy vase; 4.8h x 2.4d; D-11; "Doves, Roses, and Daisies"; TM-O, blank: 10. $25.00 – 35.00.

Plate 41. Small vase; 4.3h x 3.4d; D-11; "Doves, Roses, and Daisies"; TM-J, blank: 155. $25.00 – 35.00.

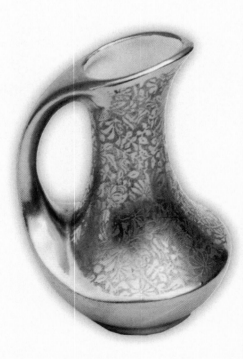

Plate 43. Round footed vase; 4.9h x 5.3d; D-11; Doves, Roses, and Daisies"; TM-G, no blank. $75.00 – 100.00.

Plate 42. Creamer or vase; 4.5h x 3d; D-11; "Doves, Roses, and Daisies"; TM-G, blank: 18. $30.00 – 50.00.

Plate 44. Two-handled vase; 6.4h x 3.4d; D-11; "Doves, Roses, and Daisies"; no trademark, no blank. $40.00 – 60.00.

Plate 45. Calla lily vase; 8.2h x 3.4d; D-11; "Doves, Roses, and Daisies"; TM-O, blank: 104. $50.00 – 75.00.

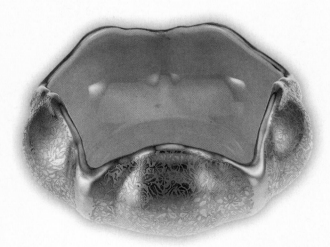

Plate 46. Lotus vase; 2.5h x 6d; D-11; "Doves, Roses, and Daisies"; TM-J, blank: 1051. Note: Cream colored inside. Plate 47 shows green inside glaze. $30.00 – 50.00.

Plate 47. Lotus bowls with green inside glaze; 2h x 4.6d, 2.7h x 6d; D-11; "Doves, Roses, and Daisies"; TM-N, TM-N, blank: 1049, 1051. Note: Green glaze. $30.00 – 50.00 each.

Plate 48. Flower bowl; 2.7h x 6.4d; D-11; "Doves, Roses, and Daisies"; no trademark, no blank. Note: black glass. $60.00 – 90.00.

Plate 49. Pansy ring bowl; 2h x 7d; D-11; "Doves, Roses, and Daisies"; TM-N; no blank. Note: The bowl can be separated into two parts. $75.00 – 110.00.

Plate 51. Bud vases; 8.2h x 2.4d, 6.2h x 2d; D-11; "Doves, Roses, and Daisies"; no trademark, no blank. Note: Similar to some Lotus glass vases. Could be "singular" items as they belonged to Lee Taylor's wife. $20.00 – 35.00 each.

Plate 50. Grecian type vase; 7h x 4.1d; D-11; "Doves, Roses, and Daisies"; TM-J, no blank. Note: Has an incised "X-4" on the bottom. $50.00 – 75.00.

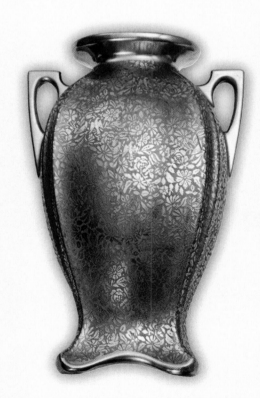

Plate 54. Gold and black vase; 7.7h x 3.3d; D-11; "Doves, Roses, and Daisies"; no trademark, no blank. Note: Probably a Central Glass blank. $125.00 – 175.00.

Plate 52. Glass bud vase; 9.7h x 2.7d; D-11; "Doves, Roses, and Daisies"; no trademark, no blank. $20.00 – 30.00.

Plate 53. AOG vase; 8.5h x 5.7d; D-11; "Doves, Roses, and Daisies"; TM-H, blank: 1050. $75.00 – 125.00.

Plate 55. Two-tier vase; 8.2h x 3.2d; D-11; "Doves, Roses, and Daisies"; TM-N, blank: 4. $75.00 – 120.00.

Plate 56. Teardrop vase; 8.3h x 4d: D-11; "Doves, Roses, and Daisies"; TM-O, blank: 103. $65.00 – 95.00.

Plate 57. Three-tier epergne; 8.2h x 9d; D-11; "Doves, Roses, and Daisies"; TM-H, no blank, Lu-Ray, Taylor, Smith and Taylor. $150.00 – 200.00.

Plate 58. Vase; 7.6h x 6l x 3w; D-11; "Doves, Roses, and Daisies"; TM-F, no blank. Note: "1-X" incised on the bottom. $75.00 – 110.00.

Plate 59. Flowered rocket vase; 7.6h x 8w; D-11; "Doves, Roses, and Daisies"; no trademark, no blank. $160.00 – 240.00.

Plate 60. Gold ball vases shown with enameled ball vase; 5.4h x 6.2d; D-11; "Doves, Roses, and Daisies"; TM-E, blank: 9002, Trenton Art Potteries (TAC). Note: Sold at Ovington's of New York. $90.00 – 130.00.

Plate 61. Bulbous vase; 4.9h x 4.7d; D-11; "Doves, Roses, and Daisies"; TM-E, blank: 630, Hall. Note: Hall trademark covered with gold. Three other examples have TM-E and one has TM-I. $45.00 – 75.00.

Plate 62. Tall, narrow vase; 8.3h x 3.5d; D-11; "Doves, Roses, and Daisies"; TM-E, blank: 631, Hall. Note: Hall trademark covered with gold. Two other examples have TM-E and one has TM-I. $40.00 – 60.00.

Plate 63. Narrow vase; 8h x 3d; D-11; "Doves, Roses, and Daisies"; TM-E, blank: 641, Hall. Note: Hall trademark covered by gold. $45.00 – 65.00.

Plate 64. Horn of plenty vase, 5.3h x 5.3w; D-11; "Doves, Roses, and Daisies"; TM-F, no blank. $80.00 – 115.00.

Plate 65. Milk "jug"; 6h x 4d; D-11; "Doves, Roses, and Daisies"; TM-N, blank: 76. $75.00 – 105.00.

Plate 66. Ball jug; 7.3h x 7d; D-11; "Doves, Roses, and Daisies"; TM-N, no blank, Hall. Note: Incised with D-7. Hall logo covered with gold. $180.00 – 250.00.

Plate 67. Modernistic pitcher; 10.2h x 4d; D-11; "Doves, Roses, and Daisies"; TM-N, blank: 6. Note: Has matching cream and sugar shown below. $80.00 – 100.00.

Plate 68. Modernistic sugar and creamer; 3.5h x 3.4l x 2.5w, 4.5h x 2.5lx 4w; D-11; "Doves, Roses, and Daisies"; TM-N, blank: 6. $35.00 – 50.00 for set.

Plate 69. Coffee pot with creamer and sugar bowl; 3.4h x 4.4l x 2.5w, 7.8h x 7.2l x 3w, 3.5h x 5l x 3w; D-11; "Doves, Roses, and Daisies"; TM-N, blank: 1253. Pot, $60.00 – 90.00; creamer and sugar, $25.00 – 45.00.

Plate 70. Comparison of sugar bowls; 3.5h x 5l x 3w, 4.5h x 5.5l x 3.2w; D-11; "Doves, Roses, and Daisies"; TM-O, TM-H, blank: both numbered 1253. Note: Different sizes were used with the same blank number. Also, different finishing techniques were used. $25.00 – 45.00 each, with creamers.

Plate 71. Coffee pot, creamer and sugar; 5.3h x 6.5l x 3.5w; 8.5h x 10l x 5w, 4.3h x 5.8l x 3w, D-11; "Doves, Roses, and Daisies"; TM-E, blank: 626, Homer Laughlin "Eggshell theme." Note: Set has a matching salt and pepper shown in Plate 133. Pot, $100.00 – 140.00; creamer and sugar, $45.00 – 70.00.

Plate 72. Coffee pot with creamer and sugar; 4h x 3.1d, 8.4h x 4.3d, 4.2h x 3.8d; D-11; "Doves, Roses, and Daisies"; TM-F, blank: 5, Steubenville Pottery Company. Pot, $70.00 – 100.00; creamer and sugar set, $30.00 – 50.00.

Plate 73. Coffee pot comparison; 8.4h x 4.3d, 7h x 4.1d; D-11; "Doves, Roses, and Daisies"; TM-F, TM-O, blank: 5, K-5, Steubenville Pottery Company. Note: The "K" model is shorter and rounder. The "K" shows that there was a change in coffee pot design for supplier "5," Steubenville Pottery Company. $70.00 – 100.00 (5), $80.00 – 110.00 (K-5).

Plate 74. Teapot, creamer and sugar; 4h x 4.6d, 6.2h x 6.2d, 3.5h x 4.1d; D-11; "Doves, Roses, and Daisies"; TM-J, TM-O, TM-J, blank: Ransom, but printed on sugar bowl, not written like others. Note the different handle shapes on the creamer and sugar in this photo and Plate 75. See Plates 209 and 210 for similar china but using D-42. $70.00 – 110.00 teapot, $40.00 – 70.00 creamer and sugar set.

Plate 75. Teapot, creamer and sugar; 4.4h x 3.7d, 7h x 6.5d, 4.2h x 4.2d; D-11; "Doves, Roses, and Daisies"; TM-E, TM-N, TM-E, blank: scripted (but each different) Ransom. Note: Not a matched set via trademarks. $70.00 – 110.00 teapot, $40.00 – 70.00 creamer and sugar set.

Plate 76. Creamer and sugar bowl; 3.6h x 3.3d, 4h x 4.5d; D-11; "Doves, Roses, and Daisies"; Both TM-K and TM-L, blank: 1960. Note: Has WDCO sticker used during WWII. $40.00 – 60.00 for the set.

Plate 77. High-handled creamer and sugar bowl; 2.9h x 3.9l x 2.3w, 3.1h x 4.8l x 2.6w; D-11; "Doves, Roses, and Daisies"; TM-E, blank: 1105. $30.00 – 50.00.

Plate 78. Small creamer and sugar; 2.5h x 2.7d, 3.5h x 3.1d; D-11; "Doves, Roses, and Daisies"; TM-F, blank: 16 (or 91). $30.00 – 55.00.

Plate 79. Creamer and sugar; 3.8h x 5l x 3w; 3h x 3.6l x 2.5w, D-11; "Doves, Roses, and Daisies"; TM-G, blank: 1726. $25.00 – 45.00.

Plate 80. Large creamer and sugar; 5h x 6.1l x 3.6w; 3.9h x 6.2l x 3.4w, D-11; "Doves, Roses, and Daisies"; TM-F, TM-E, blank: 417. $40.00 – 75.00 for pair.

Plate 81. Creamer and sugar; 4.4h x 4.7d; 3.5h x 3.8d,; D-11; "Doves, Roses, and Daisies"; TM-G, blank: 2264. $30.00 – 45.00 for the pair.

Plate 82. Creamer and sugar; 2.6h x 3.6l x 3w; 3.1h x 3.6l x 2.7w, D-11; "Doves, Roses, and Daisies"; TM-O, blank: 15. $25.00 – 40.00 per set.

Plate 83. Sugar and creamer; 4.4h x 4.3d, 3.7h x 3.5d; D-11; "Doves, Roses, and Daisies"; TM-F, TM-F, blank: 625. $30.00 – 45.00.

Plate 84. Creamer and sugar; 1.7h x 3.5d; 3.3h x 3.7d, D-11; "Doves, Roses, and Daisies"; TM-J, blank: 10. $30.00 – 45.00.

Plate 85. Creamer and sugar; 4.5h x 3.5d; 3.5h x 3d, D-11; "Doves, Roses, and Daisies"; TM-N, blank: 637, Winterling Bavaria, Germany. $30.00 – 45.00.

Plate 86. Creamer and sugar; 4h x 5.5d; 3.5h x 5.5d, D-11; "Doves, Roses, and Daisies"; TM-C, blank: 418. $35.00 – 45.00.

Plate 87. Creamer and sugar bowl; 4h x 3.3d; 3h x 3d, D-11; "Doves, Roses, and Daisies"; TM-E, blank: 13; Taylor, Smith and Taylor - Lu Ray? $45.00 – 75.00.

Plate 88. Creamer and sugar; 4h x 6d; 3h x 5.5d, D-11; "Doves, Roses, and Daisies"; TM-G, blank: 538. $30.00 – 50.00.

Plate 89. Sugar and creamer; 3.7h x 5.4l x 3.5d, 4.8h x 4.5d; D-11; "Doves, Roses, and Daisies"; blank: 360; Hutschenreuther Selb; Bottoms are marked D.11. $45.00 – 65.00.

Plate 90. Creamer and sugar bowl; 4.3h x 4.7d; 3.2h x 4.5d, D-11; "Doves, Roses, and Daisies"; TM-E, blank: 627. $40.00 – 60.00.

Plate 91. Creamer and sugar; 3.8h x 3.5d; 4h x 3.4d, D-11; "Doves, Roses, and Daisies"; TM-0, blank: K-5; Steubenville Pottery Company. $35.00 – 55.00.

Plate 92. Long service tray; 0.7h x 12.2l x 5.9w; D-11; "Doves, Roses, and Daisies"; TM-6, no blank; Royal Epiag – Made in Czechoslovakia. $75.00 – 105.00.

Plate 93. Demitasse cup and saucer; 0.6h x 4.8d; 2.3h x 2.7d, D-11; "Doves, Roses, and Daisies"; TM-F, TM-F, no blank; Similar sets have TM-J and blank number 5. $20.00 – 35.00 per set.

Plate 94. Small teacup; 1.5h x 3d; D-11; "Doves, Roses, and Daisies"; TM-I, blank: 637, Winterling Bavaria. $10.00 – 20.00; with saucer, $25.00 – 40.00.

Plate 95. Individual teapot; 5.9h x 2.9d; D-11; "Doves, Roses, and Daisies"; TM-L, no blank, Limoges, France. $45.00 – 75.00.

Plate 96. Coffee cup and saucer; 0.6h x 5.8d; 2.3h x 4d, D-11; "Doves, Roses, and Daisies"; TM-I, TM-J, blank: 650, Arzberg 473 M.I. Germany. $30.00 – 50.00.

Plate 97. Stemmed nut dish; 4h x 5.7d; D-11; "Doves, Roses, and Daisies"; no trademark, no blank; black glass. $60.00 – 95.00.

Plate 98. Pedestal nut dish; 3.5h x 6.9d; D-11; "Doves, Roses, and Daisies"; TM-F, no blank. $35.00 – 55.00.

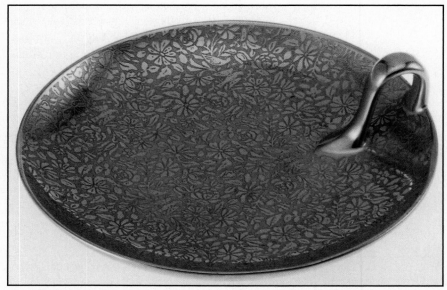

Plate 99. One-handled nappy; 0.8h x 5.7d; D-11; "Doves, Roses, and Daisies"; TM-G, no blank. $25.00 – 40.00.

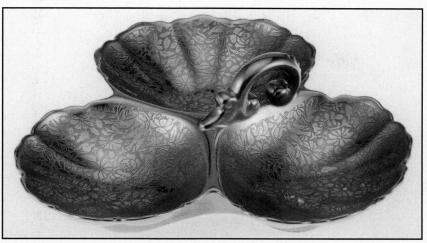

Plate 100. Three-pocket nut dish; 2h x 6.7w; D-11; "Doves, Roses, and Daisies"; TM-G, blank: 831, Czechoslovakia. $30.00 – 45.00.

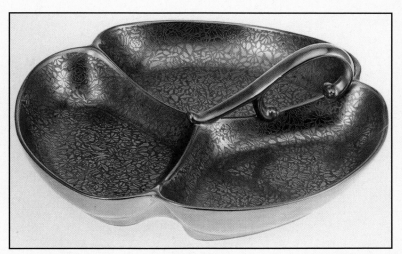

Plate 101. Handled 3-part candy dish; 2.7h x 9d; D-11; "Doves, Roses, and Daisies"; no trademark, blank: 6248. $35.00 – 55.00.

Plate 102. Dish with off-center handles; 2.3h x 6.8l x 4.5w; D-11; "Doves, Roses, and Daisies"; TM-N, blank: 19. $25.00 – 40.00.

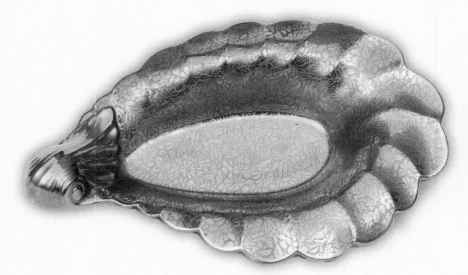

Plate 103. Shell dish; 1.5h x 9l x 6w; D-11; "Doves, Roses, and Daisies"; TM-E, blank: 12. $35.00 – 45.00.

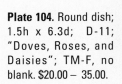

Plate 104. Round dish; 1.5h x 6.3d; D-11; "Doves, Roses, and Daisies"; TM-F, no blank. $20.00 – 35.00.

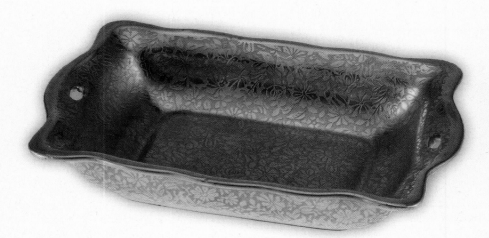

Plate 105. Pin or card dish; 1.1h x 6.4l x 4.2w; D-11; "Doves, Roses, and Daisies"; TM-G, blank: 1037. $25.00 – 40.00.

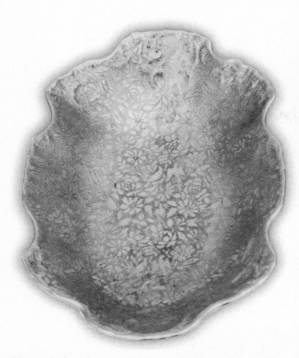

Plate 107. Heart-shaped dish; 1h x 4.9l x 4.8w; D-11; "Doves, Roses, and Daisies"; TM-O, blank: 912. $20.00 – 35.00.

Plate 106. Candy or nut dish; 1.3h x 6.6l x 4.5w; D-11; "Doves, Roses, and Daisies"; TM-N, blank: 20. $20.00 – 35.00.

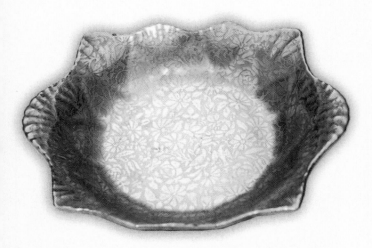

Plate 108. Two-handled small dish; 1h x 5.2l x 4.2w; D-11; "Doves, Roses, and Daisies"; TM-G, no blank. $20.00 – 35.00.

Plate 109. Circular ashtray; 1.1h x 4.1d; D-11; "Doves, Roses, and Daisies"; TM-O, blank: 205. $15.00 – 25.00.

Plate 110. Large round ashtray; 1.1h x 6.3d; D-11; "Doves, Roses, and Daisies"; TM-E, no blank. $20.00 – 35.00.

Plate 111. Vanity tray; 1h x 10.4l x 6.4w; D-11; "Doves, Roses, and Daisies"; no trademark, no blank. $25.00 – 45.00.

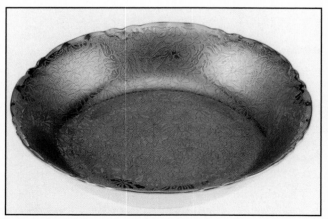

Plate 112. Small candy dish; 1.2h x 5d; D-11; "Doves, Roses, and Daisies"; TM-G, no blank; embossed with the number 13. $10.00 – 25.00.

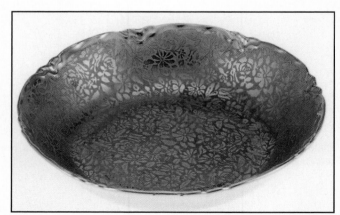

Plate 113. Round candy dish; 1.2h x 5.5d; D-11; "Doves, Roses, and Daisies"; TM-F, no blank. $25.00 – 40.00.

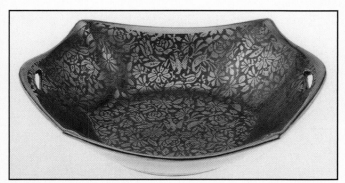

Plate 114. Candy dish; 5.5d; D-11; "Doves, Roses, and Daisies"; TM-G, blank: 1040. $20.00 – 35.00.

Plate 115. Two-handled candy dish; 1.8h x 7.3l x 6.6w; D-11; "Doves, Roses, and Daisies"; TM-H, blank: 1256. $25.00 – 40.00.

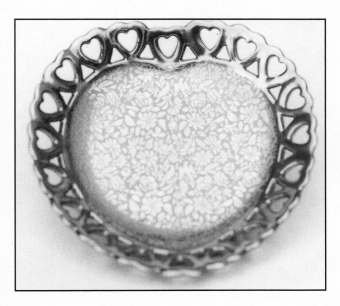

Plate 116. Bon bon dish with hearts; 1.1h x 5.7d; D-11; "Doves, Roses, and Daisies"; TM-N, blank: 28; retail sticker: S/B Lewis & Neblett in Cincinnati. $25.00 – 40.00.

Plate 117. Relish dish; 1.6h x 8.3l x 3.8w; D-11; "Doves, Roses, and Daisies"; TM-F, no blank; pottery type dish. $25.00 – 40.00.

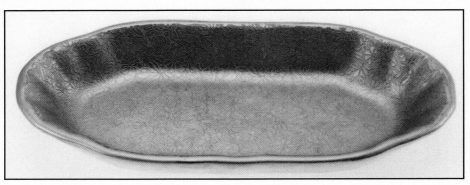

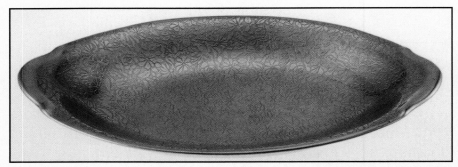

Plate 118. Relish dish; 1.1h x 9.1l x 4.8w; D-11; "Doves, Roses, and Daisies"; TM-F, blank: 2. $35.00 – 55.00.

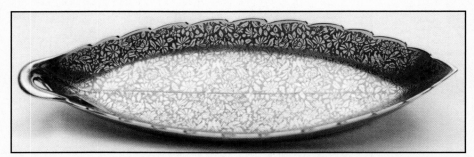

Plate 119. Leaf embossed celery dish; 1.5h x 11.2l x 4w; D-11; "Doves, Roses, and Daisies"; TM-G, blank: 4624. $35.00 – 60.00.

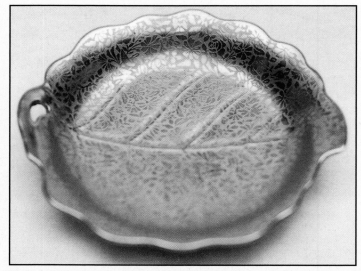

Plate 120. Small leaf patterned nappy; 1h x 5.7d; D-11; "Doves, Roses, and Daisies"; TM-N, blank: 237. $25.00 – 35.00.

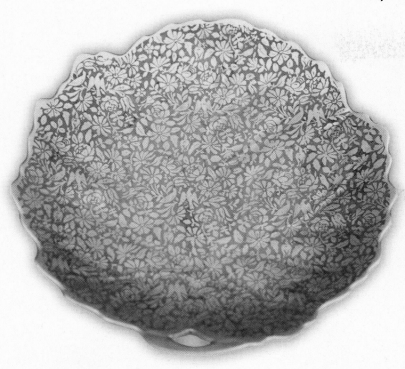

Plate 121. Veined leaf plate; 1.1h x 7d; D-11; "Doves, Roses, and Daisies"; TM-N, blank: 236. See Plate 469 for similar plate but with decal. $35.00 – 50.00.

Plate 122. Leaf veined dish; 1.1h x 7.2d; D-11; "Doves, Roses, and Daisies"; TM-N, blank: 236 1/2". The "1/2" on the back represents a slight size change in this dish. See Plate 121. $35.00 – 50.00.

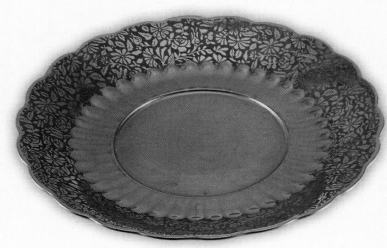

Plate 123. Bread dish?; 0.8h x 6.5d; D-11; "Doves, Roses, and Daisies"; TM-G, blank: 7066, Japan. $25.00 – 40.00.

Plate 124. Platter with two ear handles; 1h x 9.5d; D-11; "Doves, Roses, and Daisies"; no trademark, blank: 2. $40.00 – 55.00.

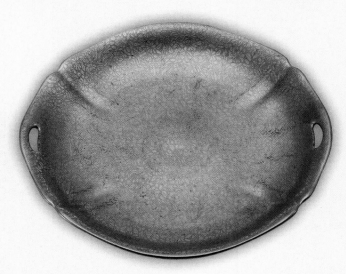

Plate 125. Plate with two small handles; 1.3h x 10.3d; D-11; "Doves, Roses, and Daisies"; no trademark, blank: 432. $40.00 – 55.00.

Plate 126. Design enlargement. Russel Wright embossed signature; scarce; made by the Steubenville Pottery Company. The Russel Wright label was used from the 1930s to about 1960. Plates 127 and 128 show two sizes of plates.

Plate 127. Small Russel Wright plate; 0.7h x 8d; D-11; "Doves, Roses, and Daisies"; TM-J, blank: 5, Steubenville, Russel Wright embossed. $55.00 – 85.00.

Plate 128. Russel Wright plate; 0.7h x 10d; D-11; "Doves, Roses, and Daisies"; TM-J or TM-N, blank: 5, Steubenville. Note: plate is fairly soft and abrades easily. $45.00 – 70.00.

Plate 129. Handled plate; 1h x 10.3d; D-11; "Doves, Roses, and Daisies"; TM-N, blank: 2; Sticker on bottom says "S/B Lewis & Neblett in Cincinnati." $45.00 – 65.00.

Plate 130. Candlestick pair; 3.3h x 4d; D-11; "Doves, Roses, and Daisies"; TM-N, blank: 914. $40.00 – 80.00.

Plate 131. Short candlesticks; 2.8h x 4.4d; D-11; "Doves, Roses, and Daisies"; no trademark, blank: 1706; marked D-11 on the bottom. $40.00 – 90.00.

Plate 132. Candlestick; 3.7h x 4.4d; D-11; "Doves, Roses, and Daisies"; TM-H, blank: 2154. $40.00 – 80.00 for a pair.

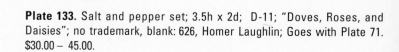

Plate 133. Salt and pepper set; 3.5h x 2d; D-11; "Doves, Roses, and Daisies"; no trademark, blank: 626, Homer Laughlin; Goes with Plate 71. $30.00 – 45.00.

Plate 134. Salt and pepper; 2.5h x 2.8d; D-11; "Doves, Roses, and Daisies"; no trademark, no blank. $30.00 – 40.00.

Plate 135. Small salt and pepper; 2.7h x 1.5d; D-11; "Doves, Roses, and Daisies"; no trademark, blank: 1202. $20.00 – 30.00.

Plate 136. Salt and pepper shakers; 3.1h x 1.3sq; D-11; "Doves, Roses, and Daisies"; no trademark, blank: 4; Marked D-11 on the bottom. $20.00 – 30.00.

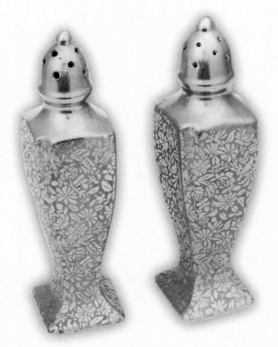

Plate 137. Tall salt and pepper; 6h x 1.7sq; D-11; "Doves, Roses, and Daisies"; no trademark, blank: 1196. $25.00 – 35.00.

Plate 138. Salt and pepper set; 6h x 2.3d; D-11; "Doves, Roses, and Daisies"; no trademark, no blank; signed "G.L.C. '57." $20.00 – 30.00.

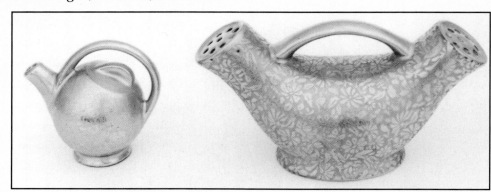

Plate 139. Small salt and combined salt and pepper; 2.2h x 1.6d, 2.6h x 5.9L; D-11; "Doves, Roses, and Daisies"; no trademark or blank for either, Japan for small salt. Small salt $25.00 – 35.00; pair $35.00 – 50.00; S&P combo $40.00 – 60.00.

Plate 140. Oval salt and pepper shakers; 5.5h x 2l x 1.5w; D-11; "Doves, Roses, and Daisies"; no trademark, blank: 1228. $25.00 – 35.00.

Plate 141. Short salt and pepper; 3.6h x 2d; D-11; "Doves, Roses, and Daisies"; no trademark, blank: 12. $20.00 – 30.00.

Plate 142. Helmet top salt and pepper; 3.4h x 1.4d; D-11; "Doves, Roses, and Daisies"; no trademark, blank: 6228. $20.00 – 30.00.

Plate 143. Acorn top salt and pepper; 4.5h x 1.6d; D-11; "Doves, Roses, and Daisies"; no trademark, blank: 204. $20.00 – 30.00.

Plate 144. Salt and pepper shakers; 4.3h x 1.7d; D-11; "Doves, Roses,"; no trademark, blank: 6218, Japan. $20.00 – 30.00.

Plate 145. Salt and pepper set; 4h x 1.6d; D-11; "Doves, Roses, and Daisies"; no trademark, blank: 601; Shakers are etched and decorated on top level area as well as the sides. $20.00 – 30.00.

Plate 146. Platinum salt and pepper; 5h x 1.5w; D-11; "Doves, Roses, and Daisies"; no trademark, blank: 203. Could be platinum or palladium; rare. $75.00 – 110.00.

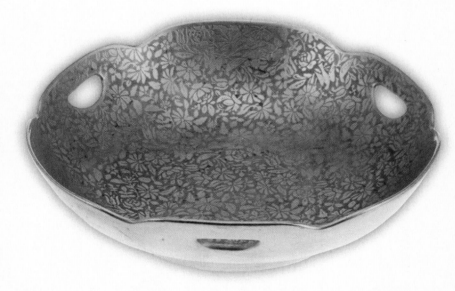

Plate 147. Small three-handled bowl; 1.6h x 6.3d; D-11; "Doves, Roses, and Daisies"; TM-F, no blank, Royal Epiag, Czechoslovakia. Signed in gold: Bessie C. Fritz. $25.00 – 40.00.

Plate 148. Very heavy bowl; 3.6h x 9.1d; D-11; "Doves, Roses, and Daisies"; TM-H, blank: 7001, Trenton Potteries (TAC). $120.00 – 160.00.

Plate 149. Heavy pottery bowl; 3h x 9.1d; D-11; "Doves, Roses, and Daisies"; TM-H, blank: 351, Trenton Potteries (TAC); Embossed with a "6" on the bottom. $110.00 – 135.00.

Plate 150. Ram's head bowl and spoon; 2.5h x 5.3d, 6.3l x 1.3d; D-11; "Doves, Roses, and Daisies"; TM-F, blank: 5606, none. $70.00 – 90.00.

Plate 151. Covered fleur-de-lis bowl with spoon; 3.5h x 7.5d, 5L x 2d; D-11; "Doves, Roses, and Daisies"; TM-G, blank: 7774, Japan. $70.00 – 90.00.

Plat 152. Black glass three-part covered dish; 5h x 6.9d; D-11; "Doves, Roses, and Daisies"; no trademark, no blank. $95.00 – 145.00.

Plate 153. Cigarette lighter; 3.3h x 3d; D-11; TM-F, no blank. $55.00 – 85.00.

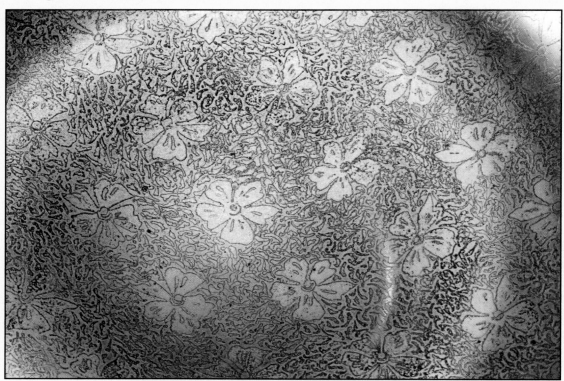

Plate 154. Design enlargement; D-12; "Aligned Periwinkle"; rare.

Plate 155. Small glass dish; 1.8h x 6.2d; D-12; "Aligned Periwinkle"; no trademark, no blank. Gold pattern is see-through on glass. $40.00 – 60.00.

Plate 156. Design enlargement; D-13; "Leaf Twisted Rope"; scarce.

Plate 157. Green ice bucket; 5.9h x 5.2d; D-13; "Leaf Twisted Rope"; no trademark, no blank. Ice bucket has 12 panels. $105.00 – 155.00.

Plate 158. Large cake plate; 2.2h x 14.2w; D-13; "Leaf Twisted Rope"; no trademark, no blank. $105.00 – 150.00.

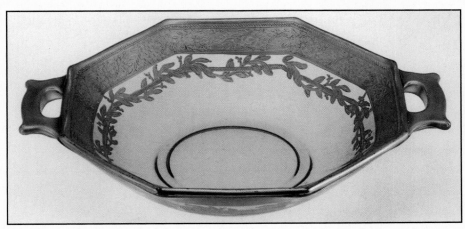

Plate 159. Two-handled dish; 1.5h x 5.9w; D-13; "Leaf Twisted Rope"; no trademark, no blank. $70.00 – 105.00.

Plate 160. "T" handle three lobe dish; 4.8h x 9.1d; D-13; "Leaf Twisted Rope"; no trademark, no blank. $85.00 – 110.00.

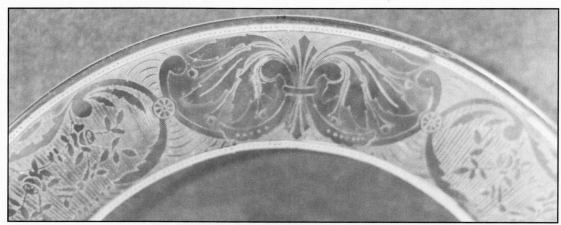

Plate 161. Design enlargement; D-14; "Headdress"; scarce availability. Notice the radial ripples from the small eight-petal flowers. D-76 is very similar.

Plate 162. Handled sandwich tray; 5h x 11.5d; D-14; "Headdress"; no trademark, no blank. Fleur-de-lis handle top. $80.00 – 120.00.

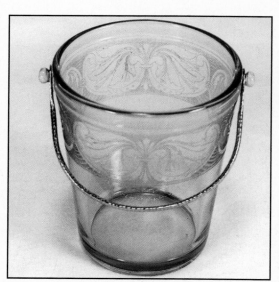

Plate 163. Pink ice bucket; 6.1h x 5.2d; D-14; "Headdress"; no trademark, no blank. Etch pattern only, no gold. Hammered silver handle. $125.00 – 175.00.

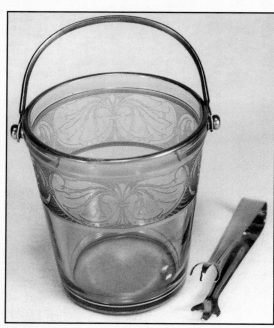

Plate 164. Pink ice bucket; 5.8h x 5.2d; D-14; "Headdress"; no trademark, no blank; etch pattern with gold dotted border. Gold handle and tongs. $140.00 – 180.00.

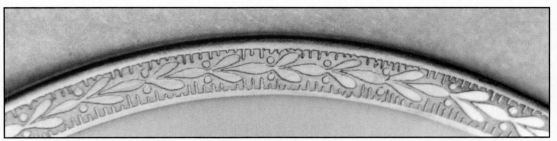

Plate 165. Design enlargement. D-16; "Leaf Formed Arrowhead Border"; scarce availability.

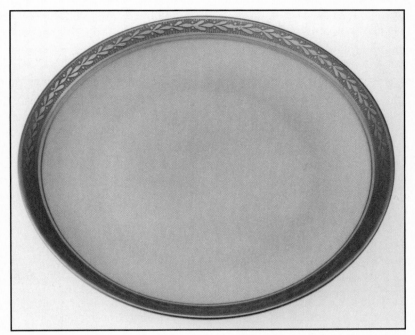

Plate 166. Bread plate; 0.7h x 6.1d; D-16; "Leaf Formed Arrowhead Border"; no trademark, no blank, Hutschenreuther Selb, Bavaria. $20.00 – 30.00.

Plate 167. Handled soup bowl; 2h x 3.2d; D-16; "Leaf Formed Arrowhead Border"; no trademark, blank: Hutschenreuther. $25.00 – 40.00.

Plate 168. Design enlargement; D-25. "Running Vine Border"; reasonable availability; Used as a stand-alone item, seldom with other patterns. One of the better wearing patterns of WDCO.

Plate 169. Sugar bowl; 2.2h x 3.4d; D-25; "Running Vine Border"; no trademark, no blank. $55.00 – 75.00 for a creamer/sugar set.

Plate 170. Ten pillow dish; 1.1h x 6.6d; D-25; "Running Vine Border"; no trademark, no blank. $35.00 – 50.00.

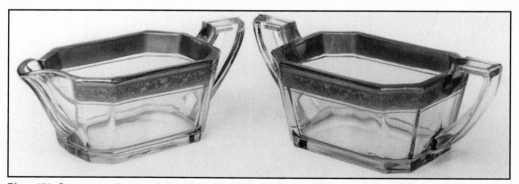

Plate 171. Creamer and sugar; 2.1h x 6l x 2.8w, 2.1h x 6.7l x 2.9w; D-25; "Running Vine Border"; no trademark, no blank. $75.00 – 95.00.

Plate 172. Very small cordial; 3h x 1.3d; D-25; "Running Vine Border"; no trademark, no blank. $30.00 – 50.00.

Plate 173. Black glass dish; 3.7h x 6.1d; D-25; "Running Vine Border"; no trademark, no blank. Glass is painted black all over. $65.00 – 85.00.

Plate 174. Covered candy dish; 3.7h x 7d; D-25; "Running Vine Border"; no trademark, blank: Heisey. $75.00 – 115.00.

Plate 175. Black glass vase; 4.5h x 6.5d; D-25; "Running Vine Border"; no trademark, no blank. $90.00 – 135.00.

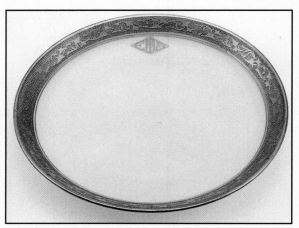

Plate 177. Bread plate; 0.7h x 6d; D-25; "Running Vine Border"; no trademark, no blank, Hutschenreuther Selb, Bavaria; This plate bears the initials "ESW." $15.00 – 25.00.

Plate 176. Tall pitcher; 8.4h x 6.4d; D-25; "Running Vine Border"; no trademark, no blank. $65.00 – 95.00.

Plate 178. Compote and plate; 2.6h x 5.4d, 1.8h x 10.5d; D-25; "Running Vine Border"; no trademark, blank: Heisey. $105.00 – 150.00.

Plate 179. Tall water pitcher; 10.2h x 5d; D-25; "Running Vine Border"; no trademark, no blank, Heisey. $125.00 – 160.00.

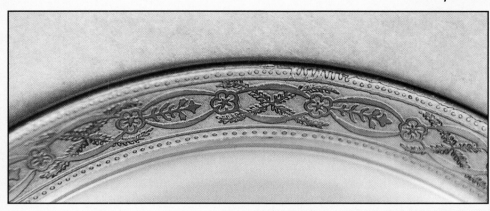

Plate 180. Design enlargement; D-30; "Flower and Ferns on Platter"; scarce availability. See D-204c items.

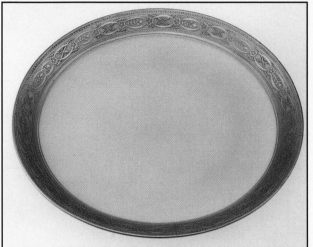

Plate 181. Bread plate; 0.7h x 6d; D-30; "Flowers and Ferns on Platters"; no trademark, no blank, Hutschenreuther, Selb, Bavaria. $20.00 – 30.00.

Plate 182. Design enlargement; D-31; "Stylized Eight Petal Flowers Separated by Diamonds"; scarce availability. Used with D-102 and as a border for other items.

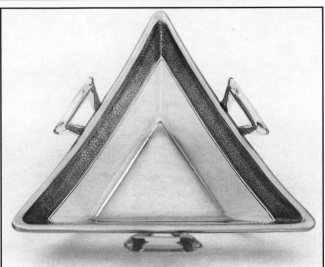

Plate 183. Triangular relish dish; 1.6h x 6.5w; D-31; "Stylized Eight Petal Flowers Separated by Diamonds"; no trademark, no blank, Heisey. $75.00 – 105.00.

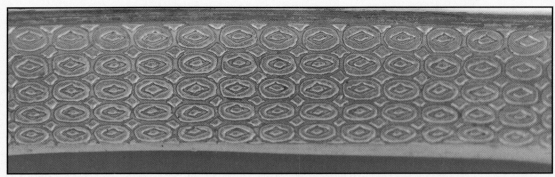

Plate 184. Design enlargement; D-33; "Stacked Ovals With Inside Diamonds"; rare. This is rare as a stand-alone item but is used as a border with other patterns.

Plate 185. Handled sandwich tray; 5h x 10d; D-33; "Stacked Ovals With Inside Diamonds"; no trademark, no blank. $65.00 – 100.00.

Plate 186. Design enlargement; D-34; "Anhingas and Urns"; scarce availability. Has interior and exterior borders of D-33.

Plate 187. Cup and saucer; 2.8h x 3.2d, 0.7h x 5.6d; D-34; "Anhingas and Urns"; TM-C, blank: Schkackean – Werth Antoinette"; D-33 borders. $60.00 – 95.00 for set.

Plate 188. Rolled lip bowl; 3.2h x 11.7d; D-34; "Anhingas and Urns"; no trademark, blank: Heisey; D-33 borders. $125.00 – 180.00.

Plate 189. Glass bread plate; 1.1h x 7.3d; D-34; "Anhingas and Urns"; no trademark, no blank. Inside and outside D-33 borders. $65.00 – 95.00.

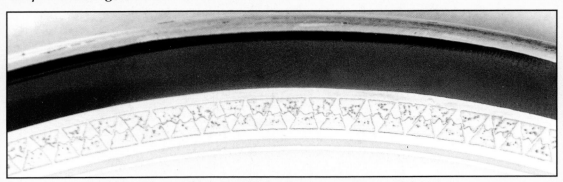

Plate 190. Design enlargement; D-35; "Up and Down Connected Arrow Points"; scarce availability. Narrow to mid-width border band.

Plate 192. Stemmed sherbet; 3.6h x 3.6d; D-35; "Up and Down Connected Arrow Points"; no trademark, no blank. Sherbet is etched with pattern said to be Tiffin Dolores. $15.00 – 25.00.

Plate 191. Blue and gold bordered plate; 0.7h x 10d; D-35; "Up and Down Connected Arrow Points"; TM-H, no blank. $30.00 – 50.00.

Plate 193. Design enlargement; D-38; "Coreopsis, Ferns, and Arbors"; scarce availability. Pattern has inside and outside border of dotted arrow points.

Plate 194. Handled sandwich plate; 5h x 11d; D-38; "Coreopsis, Ferns, and Arbors"; no trademark, no blank, Heisey. Blue flowers with turquoise ferns. $175.00 – 240.00.

Plate 195. Cream and sugar; 3.7h x 3.4d, 3.7h x 3.4d; D-38; "Coreopsis, Ferns, and Arbors"; no trademark, no blank. $65.00 – 95.00.

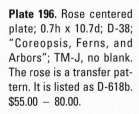

Plate 196. Rose centered plate; 0.7h x 10.7d; D-38; "Coreopsis, Ferns, and Arbors"; TM-J, no blank. The rose is a transfer pattern. It is listed as D-618b. $55.00 – 80.00.

Plate 197. Design enlargement; D-42; "Flower and Fern Filled Basket"; infrequent availability. Has stippled background. Design varies some as size of pattern changes. Almost always found on quality German china.

Plate 198. Candy dish with two handles; 2.7h x 6.7w; D-42; "Flower and Fern Filled Basket"; no trademark, blank: 1553. $75.00 – 100.00.

Plate 199. Round bowl and underplate; 2h x 4.4d, 0.6h x 5.3d; "Flower and Fern Filled Basket"; no trademark, no blank. $75.00 – 105.00.

Plate 200. Fruit dish; 2.2h x 11.5l x 7.8w; D-42; "Flower and Fern Filled Basket"; no trademark, no blank. $95.00 – 150.00.

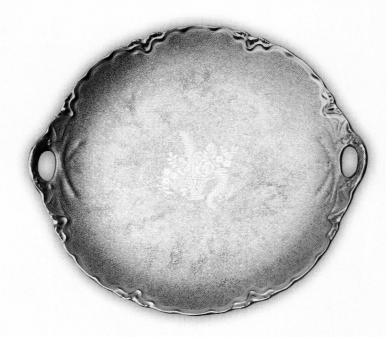

Plate 201. Serving platter; 1.1h x 10.1d; D-42; "Flower and Fern Filled Basket"; no trademark, no blank, Hutschenreuther Selb. $95.00 – 140.00.

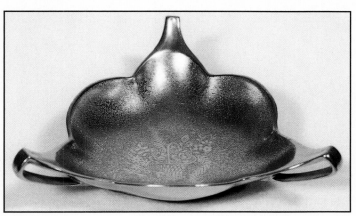

Plate 202. Triangular dish; 2.2h x 7.8w; D-42; "Flower and Fern Filled Basket"; no trademark, no blank. $85.00 – 125.00.

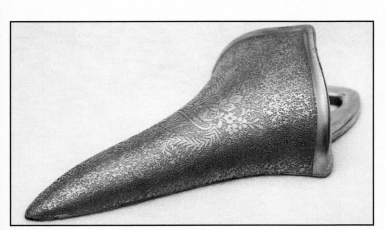

Plate 203. AOG wall pocket; 9h x 4.8w; D-42; "Flower and Fern Filled Basket"; no trademark, no blank, Eamag, Bavaria. $125.00 – 175.00.

Plate 204. Syrup pitcher; 6.5h x 9.5w; D-42; "Flower and Fern Filled Basket; no trademark, blank: 3703. $110.00 – 170.00.

Plate 205. Oval tray; 2.2h x 13l x 6w; D-42; "Flower and Fern Filled Basket"; no trademark, no blank. $105.00 – 165.00.

Plate 206. Vase; 8.3h x 4.5d; D-42; "Flower and Fern Filled Basket"; TM-H, blank: 1047. $190.00 – 250.00.

Plate 207. Salt and pepper set; 4.5h x 1.5sq; D-42; "Flower and Fern Filled Basket"; no trademark, no blank, marked Germany. There is a shift in the pattern design with the small size. $65.00 – 95.00.

Plate 208. Salt shaker; 3.1h x 1.6sq; D-42; "Flower and Fern Filled Basket"; no trademark, no blank. Pattern shift with small size. $55.00 – 75.00 for a set.

Plate 209. Cream and sugar; 4.2h x 4.1d; 4.2h x 3.7d, D-42; "Flower and Fern Filled Basket"; TM-E, Ransom. $65.00 – 100.00.

Plate 210. Creamer and sugar; 3.6h x 3d, 3.8h x 4d; D-42; "Flower and Fern Filled Basket; no trademark, Ransom, Hutschenreuther on creamer, different Hutschenreuther on sugar. $65.00 – 100.00.

Plate 211. Creamer and sugar; 2.3h x 5.3l x 3.9w; 3h x 4.7l x 2.2d, D-42; "Flower and Fern Filled Basket"; no trademark, R.S. Germany on creamer and R.S. Tillowitz on sugar. $65.00 – 100.00.

Plate 212. Creamer and sugar; 3.6h x 5.1l x 3w; 3.5h x 4.7l x 3w, D-42; "Flower and Fern Filled Basket; no trademark, blank: 2821, Hutschenreuther, Selb, Bavaria. Has "D-42" on bottom of each piece also. $65.00 – 100.00.

Plate 213. Creamer and sugar; 3.4h x 4.7l x 2.9w, 3.2h x 5.1l x 3.1w; D-42; "Flower and Fern Filled Basket; no trademark, no blank, R.S. Germany. $65.00 – 100.00.

Plate 214. Design enlargement; D-46; "Swags, Laurel Leaves and Tulips"; rare. Laurel Leaves have two to five dots behind each leaf. See also Plate 216.

Plate 215. Charger; 1.1h x 10.7d; D-46; "Swags, Laurel Leaves, and Tulips"; no trademark; no blank. Hutschenreuther Bavaria. $150.00 – 225.00.

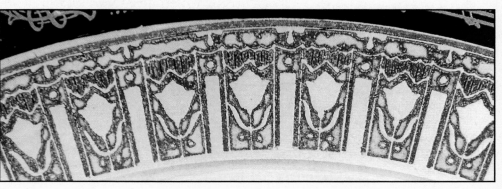

Plate 216. Design enlargement; D-46a; "Tulip Border"; scarce availability; See D-67 and D-68 for examples of use.

Plate 217. Design enlargement; D-47; "Maple Leaf and Beads (wide border)"; scarce availability; D-47a (see Plate 222) has an interior doily and more oak leaves. D-47 is a wide border and usually has transferred flowers on the interior or is plain. Considered to be one of WDCO's finer gold etch patterns.

Plate 218. Handled sandwich tray; 5.5h x 11d; D-47; "Maple Leaf and Beads (wide border)"; no trademark, no blank. Heisey. $160.00 – 250.00.

Plate 219. Plate with clear center; 1.1h x 10.6d; D-47; "Maple Leaf and Beads (wide border)"; no trademark, no blank. Hutschenreuther Selb. $140.00 – 200.00.

Plate 220. Charger; 0.7h x 10.7d; D-47; "Maple Leaf and Beads (wide border)"; TM-F, no blank. Plates with transfer center usually have a slightly lower value. Transfer is D-618a. $110.00 – 160.00.

Plate 221. Charger; 0.9h x 10.8d; D-47; "Maple Leaf and Beads (wide border)"; TM-K, no blank. Hutschenreuther "Ivory"; Has WDCO sticker from WWII era. $125.00 – 185.00.

Plate 222. Service charger; 1h x 10.5d; D-47a; "Maple Leaf and Beads (with interior doily)"; no trademark, no blank, Hutschenreuther Selb L.H.S. Bavaria. $150.00 – 210.00.

Plate 223. Design enlargement; D-51; "Drapes"; reasonable availability. The outer band of connected arrow-like leaves is not the laurel leaf pattern Series D-3.

Plate 224. Oval bowl; 3.2h x 7.7w; D-51; "Drapes"; no trademark, no blank. $65.00 – 95.00.

Plate 226. Compote base plate; 0.8h x 10d; D-51; "Drapes"; no trademark, no blank. $50.00 – 80.00.

Plate 225. Ice bucket; 6h x 5.1d; D-51; "Drapes"; no trademark, no blank. Has silver colored handle. $75.00 – 105.00.

Plate 227. Sandwich tray; 4.7h x 10.9d; D-51; "Drapes"; no trademark, no blank. $65.00 – 110.00.

Plate 228. Candy jar; 10.5h x 4.8d; D-51; "Drapes"; no trademark, no blank. $90.00 – 135.00.

Plate 229. Four compartment dish; 1.8h x 8.2d; D-51; "Drapes"; no trademark, no blank. Heisey. $60.00 – 100.00.

Plate 230. Creamer and sugar; 3.7h x 2.8d; D-51; "Drapes"; no trademark, no blank. $50.00 – 75.00.

Plate 231. Creamer and sugar; 4.2h x 4.8w; 4.2h x 4.2w, D-51; "Drapes"; no trademark, no blank. $75.00 – 105.00.

Plate 233. Black velvet bowl; 5.5h x 10.4d; D-51; "Drapes"; no trademark, no blank. $185.00 – 240.00.

Plate 232. Black glass bowl; 2.2h x 12.8d; D-51; "Drapes"; no trademark, no blank. $100.00 – 160.00.

Plate 234. Design enlargement; D-53-I; "Pheasants and Stump"; plentiful availability. Design varies from etched only to gold only to enameled colors.

Plate 235. Design enlargement; D-53-II; "Pheasants and Stump"; rare availability. Close-up of enameled pheasant.

Plate 236. Three-part dish with lid; 5.2h x 7d; D-53; "Pheasant and Stump"; no trademark, no blank. Fleur-de-lis handle, black background. $55.00 – 85.00.

Plate 237. Three-part dish with lid; 5.2h x 7d; D-53; "Pheasant and Stump"; no trademark, no blank. Amber with Fleur-de-lis lid handle. $65.00 – 100.00.

Plate 239. Oval dish with blue; 3.3h x 6.8l x 5.5w; D-53; "Pheasant and Stump"; no trademark, no blank. Heisey (Pat. 4/24/17). $50.00 – 75.00.

Plate 238. Shallow compote; 3.8h x 6.6d; D-53; "Pheasant and Stump"; no trademark, no blank. Heisey. Green glass with dimpled surface. $65.00 – 90.00.

Plate 240. Two-part green glass dish; 1.3h x 8.5l x 5.2w; D-53; "Pheasant and Stump"; no trademark, no blank. $45.00 – 75.00.

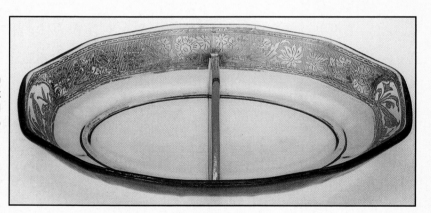

Plate 241. Celery dish; 1.6h x 12.1l x 4.7w; D-53 and D-75 combined; "Pheasant and Stump" plus "Three Birds on Hanging Vine"; no trademark, Heisey. See parrot (?) from D-75 pattern, Plate 284. $90.00 – 125.00.

Plate 242. Creamer and sugar; 4.2h x 5l x 3d, 4.2h x 4.2l x 3d; D-53; "Pheasant and Stump"; no trademark, no blank. $80.00 – 110.00.

Plate 243. Creamer and sugar; 2.7h x 6l x 3.2w; 2.7h x 5.4l x 3w; D-53; "Pheasant and Stump"; no trademark, no blank. Blue background. $55.00 – 75.00.

Plate 244. Plate with two handles; 0.8h x 6.9d; D-53; "Pheasant and Stump"; no trademark, no blank. Handle is patterned. $30.00 – 50.00.

Plate 245. Handled sandwich plate; 4.8h x 11.2d; D-53; "Pheasant and Stump"; no trademark, no blank, Heisey. $70.00 – 110.00.

Plate 246. Plate for compote; 1.2h x 11.9d; D-53; "Pheasant and Stump"; no trademark, no blank. $70.00 – 110.00.

Plate 247. Plate for compote; 0.9h x 9.7d; D-53; "Pheasant and Stump"; no trademark, no blank. $45.00 – 75.00.

Plate 248. Dish with two trays; 1.7h x 8d; D-53; "Pheasant and Stump"; no trademark, no blank. Trays are removable from dish. $65.00 – 95.00.

Plate 249. Console bowl and candlestick; 2h x 11.6d, 3.2h x 4.7d; D-53; "Pheasant and Stump"; no trademark, no blank. Etched birds with gold trim. Bowl, $75.00 – 100.00, candlesticks, $60.00 – 85.00 for pair.

Plate 250. Ice buckets; 6h x 5.1d, 3.5h x 3.3d; D-53; "Pheasant and Stump"; no trademark, no blank. Both with silver colored handles. $85.00 – 125.00, $95.00 – 135.00.

Plate 251. Candlesticks; 3.7h x 4.7d; D-53; "Pheasant and Stump"; no trademark, no blank. $90.00 – 125.00 for pair.

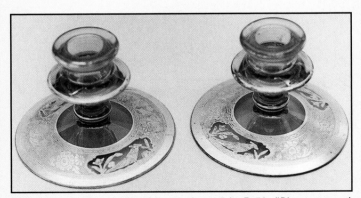

Plate 252. Amber candlesticks; 3.1h x 4.5d; D-53; "Pheasant and Stump"; no trademark, no blank. $80.00 – 110.00 a pair.

Plate 253. Amber "mushroom" bowl; 2.7h x 10.6d; no trademark, no blank. $80.00 – 110.00.

121

Plate 254. Three-part pink dish; 4.6h x 8d; D-53; "Pheasant and Stump"; no trademark, no blank. Heisey. $55.00 – 80.00.

Plate 255. Small compote and plate; 2.8h x 5.4d, 0.6h x 7.1d; D-53; "Pheasant and Stump"; no trademark, no blank. See D-53-II. Hand enameled birds. See Plate 235. $125.00 – 160.00.

Plate 256. Blue vase with brass frog; 4h x 5d; D-53; "Pheasant and Stump"; no trademark, no blank. $150.00 – 210.00.

Plate 257. Footed tumbler; 5.5h x 3.3d; D-53; "Pheasant and Stump"; no trademark, no blank. Tumbler has 12 panels and is light pink. $45.00 – 80.00.

Plate 258. Yellow glass vase; 5.3h x 7.5d; D-53; "Pheasant and Stump"; no trademark, no blank. Vase has 12 panels. $55.00 – 80.00.

Plate 259. Pink 14-panel vase; 4h x 5d; "Pheasant and Stump"; no trademark, no blank. $65.00 – 90.00.

Plate 260. Design enlargement. D-56; "Fruit Urns with 'Squared' Borders"; infrequent availability.

Plate 261. Sandwich plate; 4.9h x 11.7d; D-56; "Fruit Urns with 'Squared' Borders"; no trademark, no blank. Light yellow plate. $75.00 – 110.00.

Plate 262. Tidbit tray; 4.6h x 11.4d; D-56; "Fruit Urns with 'Squared' Borders"; no trademark, no blank. $60.00 – 100.00.

Plate 263. Demitasse cup and saucer; D-56; Cup, 2.7h x 2.5d, Saucer 0.9h x 4.6d; "Fruit Urns with 'Squared' Borders"; TM-H, no blank. $45.00 – 75.00.

Plate 264. Dolphin compote; 7.4h x 7.4d; D-56; "Fruit Urns with 'Squared' Borders"; no trademark, no blank, Heisey. $200.00 – 300.00.

Plate 265. Design enlargement; D-58; "Fox and Hounds"; infrequent availability. Has border D-3b.

Plate 266. Etched plate; 0.8h x 8.4d; D-58e; "Fox and Hounds"; no trademark, no blank. The "D-58e" means etched only - no gold or enameling. $70.00 – 110.00.

Plate 267. Hand-painted glass; 3.4h x 2.9d; D-58; "Fox and Hounds"; no trademark, no blank. $80.00 – 120.00.

Plate 268. Pink parfait glass; 8h x 2.8d; D-58; "Fox and Hounds"; no trademark, no blank. $40.00 – 65.00.

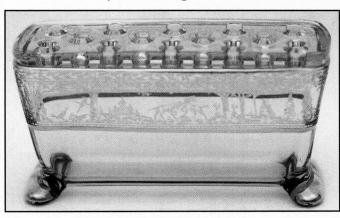

Plate 269. Pink vase with frog top; 3.6h x 7.1l x 2.5w; D-58; "Fox and Hounds"; no trademark, no blank. $175.00 – 250.00.

Plate 270. Black glass footed candy dish; 2.5h x 6.4d; D-58; "Fox and Hounds"; no trademark, no blank. $80.00 – 125.00.

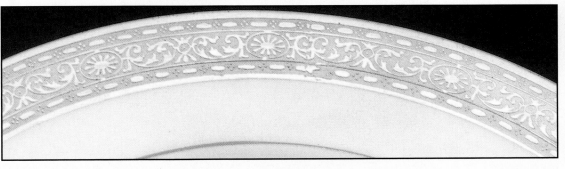

Plate 271. Design enlargement; D-61; "Encircled Twelve Petal Flowers with Dot-Dash Border"; scarce availability.

Plate 272. Bread plate; 0.7h x 6.4d; D-61; "Encircled Twelve-Petal Flowers with Dot-Dash Border"; no trademark, no blank, Hutschenreuther. $20.00 – 30.00.

Plate 273. Design enlargement; D-63; "Butterfly-like Flowers and Falling Ferns"; rare.

Plate 274. Sandwich place; 5.3h x 10.7d; D-63; "Butterfly-like Flowers and Falling Ferns"; no trademark, Heisey. $650.00 – 850.00.

Plate 275. Design enlargement; D-65; "Honeysuckle Swags with Grill Windows"; rare. Enclosed by D-36 and D-46a. D-74 is somewhat similar.

Plate 276. Decorative charger; 1h x 10.8d; D-65; "Honeysuckle Swags with Grill Windows"; no trademark, no blank. Outside border D-36, inside border D-46a. $175.00 – 225.00.

Plate 277. Design enlargement; D-67; "Short Flowered Urns with Multi-Flowered Panels"; rare. Shown with D-3b exterior border and D-46a interior border.

Plate 278. Large serving platter; 0.7h x 12.7d; D-67; "Short Flowered Urns with Multi-Flowered Panels; no trademark, no blank. Has D-3b exterior and D-46a interior border. $400.00 – 600.00.

Plate 279. Sandwich tray; 5h x 11.7d; D-67; "Short Flowered Urns with Multi-Flowered Panels"; no trademark, no blank. Has borders D-3b and D-46a. $400.00 – 700.00.

Plate 280. Design enlargement; D-68; "Checkered Flags and Sprays"; rare; D-36 and D-46a enclose D-68.

Plate 281. Charger; 1.1h x 10.6d; D-68; "Checkered Flags and Sprays"; no trademark, no blank, Royal Bavarian Hutschenreuther. Bounded by D-36 and D-46a. $150.00 – 225.00.

Plate 282. Design enlargement; D-74; "Nymphs Holding Garlands"; rare. Shown example is bounded by D-36 and D-46a.

Plate 283. Decorative plate; 1.1h x 10.5d; D-74; "Nymphs Holding Garlands"; no trademark, no blank. Bounded by D-36 and D-46a. $175.00 – 250.00.

Plate 285. Champagne glass; 5.4h x 4.2d; D-75; "Three birds on hanging vine"; no trademark, no blank. $35.00 – 55.00.

Plate 284. Design enlargement; D-75; "Three birds on hanging vine"; scarce availability.

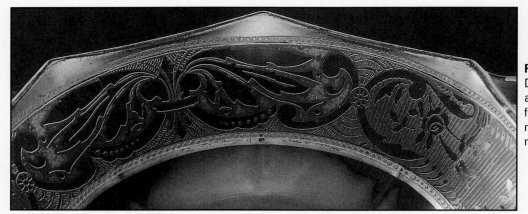

Plate 286. Design enlargement; D-76; "Headdress II"; scarce availability. Similar to D-14 but fewer radial lines. Imitations do not have complete radial circles near round flower.

Plate 287. Green two-handled dish; 1.7h x 7.3l x 5.9w; D-76; "Head-dress II"; no trademark, no blank. Similar to D-14. $40.00 – 65.00.

Plate 288. Small candy dish; 1.7h x 7.3l x 5.9w; D-76; "Headdress II"; no trademark, no blank. Plate 287 shows a different decorating scheme and green glass. $40.00 – 65.00.

Plate 289. Sherbet dish; 4.1h x 4d; D-76; "Head-dress II"; no trademark, no blank. $40.00 – 65.00.

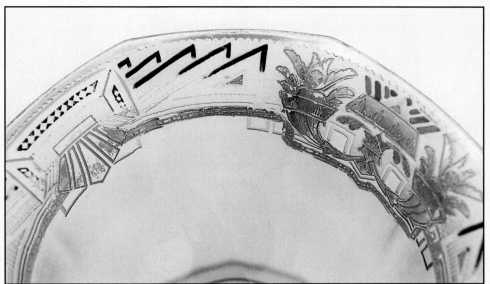

Plate 290. Design enlargement; D-78; "Aztec Triangles Five"; scarce availability.

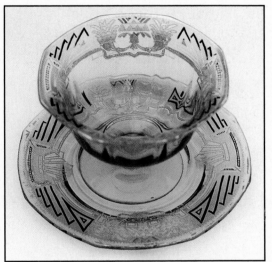

Plate 291. Compote and under plate; 4.1h x 5.5d, 0.6h x 7.4d; D-78; "Aztec Triangles Five"; no trademark, no blank. Yellow glass with eight panels on compote. Part of etched surface undecorated. $85.00 – 125.00.

Plate 292. Condiment dish with plate; 3h x 5.3d, 1h x 11.4d; D-78; "Aztec Triangles Five"; no trademark, no blank. Green glass with parts of the etched surface left undecorated. $80.00 – 120.00.

Plate 293. Three-part covered dish; 5.3h x 7.2d; D-78; "Aztec Triangles Five"; no trademark, no blank. Parts of etched surface left undecorated. $90.00 – 130.00.

Plate 294. Design enlargement; D-90; "Border of Semicircles and Arrow Points"; reasonable availability. Stand-alone border seen on etch plate tracing.

Plate 295. Design enlargement; D-90a; "Mixed Flowers, Fruit and Leaves"; scarce availability. Pattern is surrounded by D-90 borders.

Plate 296. Design enlargement; D-90b; "Rose Buds and Ten Petal Flower"; rare. Surrounded by D-90 border.

Plate 297. Eight-panel footed bowl; 7.2h x 9.5d; D-90b; "Rose Buds and Ten-Petal Flowers"; no trademark, no blank. With D-90 borders. $85.00 – 115.00.

Plate 298. Design enlargement; D-90c; "Leafed Plumes With Windows"; reasonable availability. Interior and exterior D-90 borders.

Plate 299. Demitasse cup and saucer; 2.3h x 2.2d, 0.7h x 4.5d; D-90c; "Leafed Plumes with Windows"; TM-G, no blank. Bounded by D-90 border. $20.00 – 35.00.

Plate 300. Small plate; 1.1h x 7.5d; D-90c; "Leafed Plumes with Windows"; TM-J, no blank. Bounded by D-90. $50.00 – 75.00.

Plate 301. Soup bowl and saucer; 0.8h x 6.2d; 1.8h x 4.7d; D-90c; "Leafed Plumes with Windows"; TM-H, no blank. D-90 borders. $25.00 – 40.00.

Plate 302. Design enlargement; D-90d; "Alyssums"; scarce availability. With D-90 and D-90a borders.

Plate 303. Bluish charger; 0.8h x 10.9d; D-90d; "Alyssums"; TM-H, blank: 359. Has number "359" printed on the bottom, not hand painted as is usual. Shown with a typical "transfer" floral arrangement and D-90 and D-90a. $65.00 – 85.00.

Plate 304. Design enlargement; 90e; "Doubled Leafed Plums with Windows"; scarce availability. A compound pattern with D-90, D-90c, D-90a, D-90, and again D-90c, starting at the outside edge.

Plate 305. Decorative plate; 1.1h x 10.5d; D-90e; "Doubled Leafed Plumes with Windows"; TM-H, no blank. $70.00 – 100.00.

Plate 306. Design enlargement; D-92; "Scrolls with Kite and Dangling Flowers"; scarce availability. This is primarily a transfer pattern.

Plate 307. Demitasse cup and saucer; 0.8h x 4.8d; 2.4h x 2.5d, D-92; "Scrolls with Kites and Dangling Flowers"; no trademark, TM-J; no blank, for either. $20.00 – 30.00.

Plate 308. Design enlargement; D-97; "Etched Poinsettias, Panel, and Coral Bell Border"; rare. Used transfer decal No. 02678 (Schulenburg). Panel is usually filled with transfer of flower arrangement.

Plate 309. Charger; 0.9h x 10.6d; D-97; "Etched Poinsettias, Panel, and Coral Bell Border"; TM-H, no blank. $120.00 – 165.00.

Plate 310. Design enlargement; D-100a; "Swinging Nymphs and Potted Plants"; rare. Enclosed by Hobart etching D-6 on outside. Interior border unnumbered.

Plate 311. China charger; 1.1h x 10.6d; D-100a; "Swinging Nymphs and Potted Plants"; no trademark, no blank, Crown Lion Ivory Hutschenreuther; Has D-6 outside border. $150.00 – 225.00.

Plate 312. Design enlargement; D-100b; "Swinging Nymphs and Potted Plants"; rare. Enclosed by D-8.

Plate 313. Glass charger; 0.7h x 10.4d; D-100b; "Swinging Nymphs and Potted Plants"; no trademark, no blank. Outside border of D-8. Design is on a glass plate and is less common. $175.00 – 250.00.

Plate 314. Design enlargement; D-101; Greek Key border; plentiful availability. Also used in D-125 series.

Plate 315. Cup and saucer; D-101; "Greek Key Border"; no trademark, no blank; Hutschenreuther Selb Bavaria. Also used in D-125 series. Used often by WDCO but also by others. This cup and saucer many not be WDCO. $15.00 – 25.00.

Plate 316. Design enlargement; D-101a; "Encircled Flower Basket"; scarce availability. With D-101 border. This design pattern often shows severe darkening.

Plate 317. Handled dish with blue border; 1.7h x 7.3d; D-101a; "Encircled Flower Basket"; no trademark, Heisey. With D-101 border. $70.00 – 110.00.

Plate 318. Creamer/sugar with green; 5.1h x 3.8d; 4.3h x 3.2d; D-101a; "Encircled Flower Basket"; no trademark, no blank. Heisey. With Greek Key border, D-101. $90.00 – 135.00.

Plate 319. Green rimmed candy dish; 9.3h x 3.9w; D-101a; "Encircled Flower Basket"; no trademark, no blank. Uses D-101 Greek Key border. $80.00 – 135.00.

Plate 320. Design enlargement; D-102; "Latticed Vines"; rare. Outside border is D-31.

Plate 321. Three-footed bowl; 3.5h x 11.8d; D-102; "Latticed Vines"; no trademark, no blank. Border is D-31. $80.00 – 125.00.

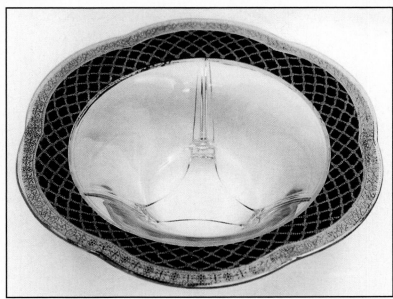

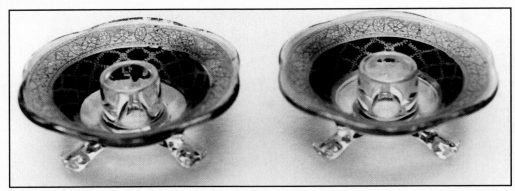

Plate 322. Three-footed candlesticks; 1.6h x 4.5d; D-102; "Latticed Vines"; no trademark, no blank. Uses D-31 border. $40.00 – 65.00 for pair.

Plate 323. Design enlargement; D-125a; "Double Connected Roses"; reasonable availability. With D-101 border. Roses connected by double stems. Two small blue flowers usually between pairs of roses.

Plate 324. Bowl; 1.2h x 8.3d; D-125a; "Double Connected Roses"; no trademark, no blank. With D-101 border. $40.00 – 65.00.

Plate 325. Celery dish; 9.3l x 3.5w; D-125a; "Double Connected Roses"; no trademark, no blank. Heisey. With D-101 border. $35.00 – 60.00.

Plate 326. French dressing boat; 3.2h x 5.9l x 3.2w; D-125a; "Double Connected Roses"; no trademark, no blank. Uses Greek Key D-101 border. $55.00 – 75.00.

Plate 327. One-pound candy jar; 10.4h x 4.5d; D-125a; "Double Connected Roses"; no trademark, no blank. With D-101 border. $85.00 – 130.00.

Plate 328. Cruet; 6.9h x 4d; D-125a; "Double Connected Roses"; no trademark, no blank. Heisey. With D-101 border. $260.00 – 340.00.

141

Plate 329. Design enlargement; D-125b; "Double Connected Flowers"; scarce availability; D-101 border. Often done in purple, orange, or yellow flowers.

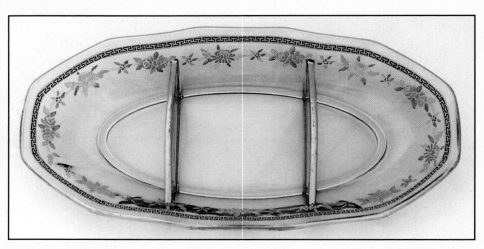

Plate 330. Three-part green dish; 1.5h x 11.8l x 5.8w; D-125b; "Double Connected Flowers"; no trademark, no blank. D-101 border. $45.00 – 80.00.

Plate 331. Candlesticks; 2.3h x 4.8d; D-125b; "Double Connected Flowers"; no trademark, no blank. D-101 border. $65.00 – 95.00 per pair.

Plate 332. Console bowl; 2.8h x 11.9d; D-125b; "Double Connected Flowers"; no trademark, no blank. Uses D-101 Greek Key border. $85.00 – 135.00.

Plate 333. Design enlargement; D-127-I; "Large Gold Daisy and Silver Urn"; scarce availability. Daisy is yellow-gold with reddish-orange center.

Plate 334. Design enlargement; D-127-II; "Large Gold Daisy and Silver Urn"; scarce availability. Silver urn has two small blue flowers on top of it. D-127-I and D-127-II are usually combined as D-127.

Plate 335. Oval bowl; 3h x 9.4l x 8w; D-127; "Large Gold Daisy and Silver Urn"; no trademark, no blank. Heisey (Patent 4/24/17). $85.00 – 105.00.

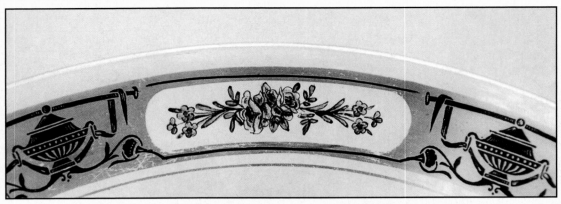

Plate 336. Design enlargement; D-133; "Draped Covered Urn with Flowers"; scarce availability.

Plate 337. Dish with ten panels; 1.3h x 6.6d; D-133; "Draped Covered Urn with Flowers"; no trademark, no blank. Heisey (?). $75.00 – 115.00.

Plate 338. Oval bowl; 3.1h x 9.5l x 7.9w; D-133; "Draped Covered Urn with Flowers"; no trademark, no blank, Heisey (Pat 4/27/17). $100.00 – 140.00.

Plate 339. Celery dish; 1.7h x 12l x 4.7w; D-133; "Draped Covered Urn with Flowers"; no trademark, no blank, Heisey. Notice lengthening of flowers. $110.00 – 155.00.

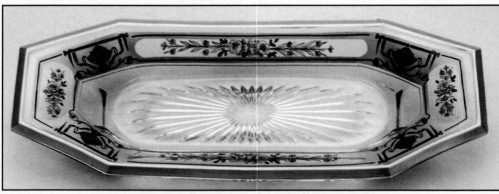

Plate 340. Celery dish; 7h x 12.5l x 5.5w; D-133; "Draped Covered Urn with Flowers"; no trademark, no blank, Heisey. $60.00 – 90.00.

Plate 341. Small compote; 3.9h x 5.7d; D-133; "Draped Covered Urn with Flowers"; no trademark, no blank. $110.00 – 155.00.

Plate 342. Design enlargement; D-137; "Wreath-Enclosed Flower with Shark Tooth Border"; rare.

Plate 343. Sandwich tray; 5h x 10.5d; D-137; "Wreath-Enclosed Flower with Shark Tooth Border"; no trademark, no blank, Heisey. $110.00 – 160.00.

Plate 344. Luncheon plate; 1.1h x 8.6d; D-137; "Wreath-Enclosed Flower with Shark Tooth Border"; no trademark, no blank, Heisey (?). $45.00 – 85.00.

Plate 345. Glass candle holder; 3.2h x 4.5d; D-137; "Wreath-Enclosed Flower with Shark Tooth Border"; no trademark, no blank, Heisey (?). $90.00 – 125.00 per pair.

Plate 346. Design enlargement; D-153; "Impatiens with Squiggles"; infrequent availability.

Plate 347. Twisting salt and pepper; 3.6h x 1.6w; D-153; "Impatiens with Squiggles"; no trademark, blank: 312 (Japan). $25.00 – 35.00.

Plate 349. Divided candy dish; 8l x 5w; D-153; "Impatiens with Squiggles"; TM-G; blank: 5. $45.00 – 65.00.

Plate 348. Two salts?; 6h x 1.6sq; D-153; "Impatiens with Squiggles (on left); no trademark, no blank. Purchased as a pair but one is D-153 and the other, D-11, is darker gold. $30.00 – 40.00 per pair.

Plate 350. Bon bon dish; 1.4h x 9l x 5.5w; D-153; "Impatiens with Squiggles"; TM-H, blank: 509. $65.00 – 80.00.

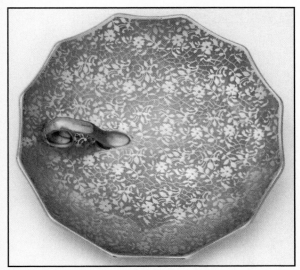

Plate 351. One-handled nappy; 1.3h x 6d; D-153; "Impatiens with Squiggles"; TM-H; blank: 603. $45.00 – 65.00.

Plate 352. Ikebana or Moribana flower dish; 2h x 9.8w x 8.6l; D-153; "Impatiens with Squiggles"; TM-F, blank: 9037, Trenton Potteries Company (TAC). $125.00 – 160.00.

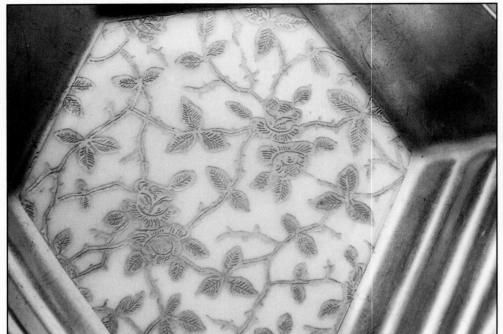

Plate 353. Design enlargement; D-169; "Twigs, Leaves, and Roses"; infrequent availability.

Plate 354. Creamer and sugar; 4h x 4.5l, 3h x 3.5l; D-169; "Twigs, Leaves, and Roses"; TM-G, blank: 5998. $50.00 – 75.00.

Plate 355. Tea set; 4.5h x 4.4d, 6.5h x 7.5d, 3.5h x 5d; D-169; "Twigs, Leaves, and Roses; TM-H, blank: 297. $95.00 – 140.00 for three-piece set.

Plate 356. Urn style vase; 7.9h x 2.9d; D-169; "Twigs, Leaves, and Roses"; TM-G, blank: 418. $80.00 – 120.00.

Plate 357. Vase with four feet; 4.6h x 3.5l x 1.8w; D-169; "Twigs, Leaves, and Roses"; TM-H, no blank. $65.00 – 95.00.

Plate 358. Gold and white vase; 8.5h x 5.7d; D-169; "Twigs, Leaves, and Roses"; TM-H, blank: 1050. See Plate 53. $85.00 – 140.00.

Plate 359. Ewer; 5.7h x 3.3l x 2w; D-169; "Twigs, Leaves, and Roses"; TM-G, blank: 680. $75.00 – 100.00.

Plate 360. Dish, six-sided; 1.1h x 6.0w; D-169; "Twigs, Leaves, and Roses;" TM-H, blank: 256. $45.00 – 75.00.

Plate 361. Dish with three handles; 1.5h x 7.2d; D-169; "Twigs, Leaves, and Roses"; TM-H, blank: 1260. $70.00 – 100.00.

Plate 362. Design enlargement; D-204c; "Griffins Smelling Flowers"; rare. Generally associated with Central Glass of Wheeling and is called "Harding" etching. Pattern is clearly presented as D-204c. Did WDCO do the etching? Maybe they did even after Central Glass closed and sold their molds to Imperial Glass in 1939. Gold border D-30.

Plate 363. Glass bread plate; 0.8h x 7.2d; D-204c; "Griffins Smelling Flowers"; no trademark, no blank. Border is D-30. $40.00 – 75.00.

Plate 364. Various Griffin glasses; left to right, 6.5h x 4d, 6.5h x 2.8d, 5.3h x 2.8d, 7.5h x 4d; D-204c; "Griffins Smelling Flowers"; no trademark, no blank, Central Glass. President Harding supposedly bought a 300-piece set of this pattern, but gold encrusted. These may not have been etched by WDCO. Pattern is slightly different from D-204c. $60.00 – 80.00 each.

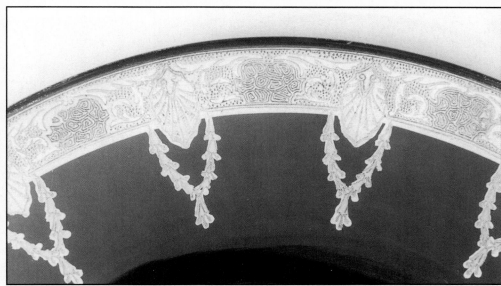

Plate 365. Design enlargement; D-204g; "Hanging Garlands and Shields"; scarce availability.

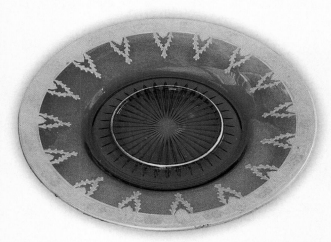

Plate 366. Blue and gold compote plate; 0.8h x 10d; D-204g; "Hanging Garlands and Shields"; no trademark, no blank. Heisey? $95.00 – 140.00.

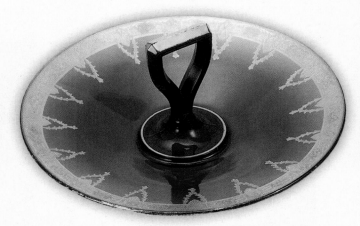

Plate 367. Tidbit tray with handle; 4.5h x 10.3d; D-204g; "Hanging Garlands and Shields"; no trademark, no blank. $85.00 – 120.00.

Plate 368. Sherbet dish; 4.3h x 3.7d; D-204g; "Hanging Garland and Shields"; no trademark, no blank. $30.00 – 50.00.

Plate 369. Juice glass; 3.7h x 2d; D-256; "A Single Orange"; no trademark, no blank. There may be others in this series. $35.00 – 50.00.

Plate 370. Design enlargement; D-298; "Sixes or Nines with Flowers"; rare. If etched pattern is placed on the underside of a glassware item, the "6" or "9" will be backwards. Shown pattern comes from WDCO Design Book.

Plate 371. Plate, with two handles; 1.8h x 7.1d; D-298; "Sixes or Nines with Flowers"; no trademark, no blank, Imperial Glass Company - Candlewick. $70.00 – 110.00.

Plate 372. Large fruit bowl; 3.1h x 15.8d; D-298; "Sixes or Nines with Flowers"; no trademark, no blank. Etched pattern. $95.00 – 130.00.

Plate 373. Fish glass; 2.9h x 2.1d; D-301; "Red and Black Laughing Fish"; no trademark, no blank; rare. Other not shown but related items: D-302, "Fish Eyes," D-311, "Seven Arm Octopus." $55.00 – 95.00 each.

Plate 374. Design enlargement; D-320d; "Meissen Flowers"; infrequent availability. Enlargement of the pattern from the WDCO Design Book.

Plate 375. Creamer; 3.2h x 2.7sq; D-320d; "Meissen Flowers"; TM-G, blank: 1724. $35.00 – 65.00 for creamer and sugar.

Plate 376. Urn type vase; 7.8h x 3.7d; D-320d; "Meissen Flowers"; TM-G, blank: 8674. $65.00 – 105.00.

Plate 377. Creamer and sugar; 4.5h x 4w x 4.7l; 3.3h x 3.3w x 3.8l; D-320d; "Meissen Flowers"; TM-G, blank: 9216. $60.00 – 80.00.

Plate 378. Decanter with mallard; 12.6h x 5d; D-486a; "Game Birds - Mallard"; no trademark, no blank. $75.00 – 125.00.

Plate 379. Game Bird martini glasses; 3.5h x 3.8d; D-486b, c, e; "Game Birds - Various"; no trademark, no blank. $15.00 – 25.00 each.

Plate 380. Game Bird martini glasses; 3.5h x 2.8d; D-486 a, d, f; "Game Birds - Various"; no trademark, no blank. $15.00 – 25.00 each.

Plate 381. Game Bird martini glass; 3.5h x 2.8d; D-486k; "Game Birds - Sage Hen." No trademark, no blank. $20.00 – 30.00.

Plate 382. Game Bird glasses; 3.5h x 2.8d, 3.3h x 2.9d; D-486e; "Game Birds - Blue Goose"; no trademark, no blank. Same bird but different artists. $15.00 – 25.00 each.

Plate 383. "V" glasses; 3.6h x 2.8d; D-486a, h; "Game Birds - Mallard and Mountain Quail"; no trademark, no blank. $20.00 – 30.00 each.

Plate 384. Turkey and Bob White glasses; 5.6h x 2.8d; D-486j, c; "Game Birds - Wild Turkey and Bob White"; no trademark, no blank. The Turkey and the Sage Hen appear to be the least common series "A" birds. $20.00 – 30.00 each.

Plate 385. Grouse ashtray; 0.7h x 6.1d; D-486i; "Game Birds - Ruffed Grouse"; TM-J, no blank. $25.00 – 35.00.

Plate 386. Duck ashtray; 0.7h x 6.1d; D-486g; "Game Birds - Pintail Duck"; TM-J, no blank. $20.00 – 30.00.

Plate 387. Martini pitchers; 9.1h x 4.4d; D-486f, a; "Game Birds - Ring Necked Pheasant, Mallard"; no trademark, no blank. $75.00 – 105.00 each.

Plate 388. Pheasant bird plate; 0.6h x 8.1d; D-486f; "Game Birds - Ring Necked Pheasant"; TM-M, no blank, Homer Laughlin theme. $20.00 – 30.00.

Plate 389. Mallard plate; 0.6h x 8.1d; D-486a; "Game Birds - Mallard"; TM-M, no blank, Homer Laughlin theme. $20.00 – 30.00.

Plate 390. Red-headed duck plate; 0.6h x 8.1d; D-486d; "Game Birds - Red-headed Duck"; TM-M, no blank, Homer Laughlin theme. $20.00 – 30.00.

Plate 391. Blue goose plate; 0.6h x 8.1d; D-486e; "Game Birds - Blue Goose"; TM-M, no blank, Homer Laughlin theme. $20.00 – 30.00.

Plate 392. Mountain quail plate; 0.6h x 8.1d; D-486h; "Game Birds - Mountain Quail"; TM-M, no blank, Homer Laughlin theme; $20.00 – 30.00.

Plate 393. Bob White plate; 0.6h x 8.1d; D-486c; "Game Birds - Bob White"; TM-M, no blank, Home-Laughlin theme. $20.00 – 30.00.

Plate 394. Ruffed grouse plate; 0.6h x 8.1d; D-486i; "Game Birds - Ruffed Grouse"; TM-M, no blank, Homer Laughlin theme. $20.00 – 30.00.

Plate 395. Prairie chicken plate; 0.6h x 8.1d; D-486l; "Game Birds - Prairie Chicken"; TM-M, no blank, Homer Laughlin theme. $20.00 – 30.00.

Plate 396. Gold mallard plate; 0.7h x 8.4d; D-486a; "Game Birds - Mallard"; TM-J, no blank. $65.00 – 95.00.

Plate 397. Gold blue goose plate; 0.7h x 8.4d; D-486e; "Game Birds - Blue Goose"; TM-J, no blank. $65.00 – 95.00.

Plate 398. Gold ring neck pheasant plate; 0.7h x 8.4d; D-486f; "Game Birds - Ring Neck Pheasant"; TM-J, no blank. $65.00 – 95.00.

Plate 399. Gold sage hen plate; 0.7h x 8.4d; D-486k; "Game Birds - Sage Hen"; TM-J, no blank. $65.00 – 95.00.

Plate 400. Ring neck pheasant plate; 0.7h x 8.4d; D-486f; "Game Birds - Ring Necked Pheasant"; TM-J, no blank. $20.00 – 30.00.

Plate 401. Mallard decanter; 8.5h x 5.7l x 3.3w; D-486a; "Game Birds - Mallard"; no trademark, no blank. $85.00 – 125.00.

Plate 402. Church plate; 0.8h x 10d; D-600a; "Pictorial Church Item - North Broadway Methodist Church, Columbus, Ohio"; TM-J, no blank. $10.00 – 25.00.

Plate 403. Church plate; 0.8h x 10d; D-600b; "Pictorial Church Item - Dillon Chapel Methodist Church"; TM-J, no blank. $10.00 – 25.00.

Plate 404. Church plate; 0.8h x 10d; D-600c; "Pictorial Church Item - Broad Street Methodist Church, Columbus, Ohio"; TM-J, no blank. $10.00 – 25.00.

Plate 405. Church plate; 0.8 x 10d; D-600d; "Pictorial Church Item - Washington Cathedral"; TM-J, no blank, Steubenville. Marked Adam Antiques, Steubenville. $10.00 – 25.00.

Plate 406. Church plate; 0.8h x 9.9d; D-600e; "Pictorial Church Item - The Franklin Street Methodist Church, Johnstown, Pennsylvania"; TM-J, no blank, Homer Laughlin. $10.00 – 25.00.

Plate 407. Church plate; 0.9h x 10.1d; D-600f; "Pictorial Church Item, Gatonsville United Methodist, MD"; TM-M, no blank, Homer Laughlin theme, J46, N6. Plate information on the back, 1946. $10.00 – 25.00.

Plate 408. Church plate; 0.9 x 9.8d; D-600g; "Pictorial Church Item - Trinity Methodist Church, Columbus, OH"; TM-J, no blank, Homer Laughlin theme, 1951. $10.00 – 25.00.

Plate 409. Church plate; 0.9 x 9.9d; D-600h; "Pictorial Church Item - St. Stephen's Evangelical and Reformed Church, Sandusky, Ohio"; no trademark, no blank, Homer Laughlin theme. 1957. $10.00 – 25.00.

Plate 410. School mug; 5.2h x 3.7d; D-602; "School Related Items - Cornell University"; TM-J, no blank, Hall. $10.00 – 25.00.

Plate 411. School plate; 0.8h x 9.9d; D-602a; "School Related Items - Barboursville High School, WV"; TM-J, no blank, Homer Laughlin theme, C52N5, 1952. $10.00 – 30.00.

Plate 412. State plate; 0.9h x 10d; D-604a; "Pictorial State Items - Oklahoma"; TM-J, no blank, Homer Laughlin, 1958. $10.00 – 25.00.

Plate 413. State plate; 1h x 10.1d; D-604b; "Pictorial State Items - Mississippi"; TM-J, no blank. $10.00 – 25.00.

Plate 414. State plate; 1h x 10.1d; D-604d; "Pictorial State Items - Virginia"; TM-J, no blank. $10.00 – 25.00.

Plate 415. Plate of home; 1.1h x 10.5d; D-606a; "Pictorial Family Items - Unknown Home"; no trademark, no blank. House is bounded by D-90a and D-90c. While probably not a "singular" item, this plate and any matching pieces probably went only to one family. $100.00 – 125.00.

Plate 416. Souvenir state coasters; 0.5h x 3.9d; D-604e, D-604f; "Pictorial State Items, a) West Virginia, b) Pennsylvania; TM-J, no blank; reasonable. $15.00 – 30.00.

Plate 418. Port of New York ashtray; 1.2h x 7.3sq; D-610a; "Organizational Items - Maritime Association"; TM-J, no blank. $10.00 – 25.00.

Plate 417. Historical plate; 0.8h x 9.3d; D-608a; "Pictorial Historical Items - Twin Tunnels - Pennsylvania Turnpike"; TM-M, no blank, Homer Laughlin. $10.00 – 25.00.

Plate 419. Schaefer beer mug; 5.6h x 3.8d; D-612a; "Event Celebrations - Schaefer Beer 1952"; TM-J, no blank. $20.00 – 30.00.

Plate 420. Design enlargement; D-618a; "Typical Floral Transfer Patterns for Plates"; reasonable availability. Many different transfer patterns were used by WDCO for plate centers. The design was used on some of the D-47 series.

Plate 421. Wall pockets; 7.3h x 3.4w; D-621d, e; "Small Birds - Red Cardinal, Blue Grosbeak"; no trademark, no blank. $85.00 – 110.00 each.

Plate 422. Grosbeak bird plate; 0.8h x 7.9d; D-621e; "Small Birds - Blue Grosbeak"; TM-J, no blank. $30.00 – 45.00.

Plate 423. Java bird plate; 0.8h x 7.9d; D-621g; "Small Birds - Java SP"; TM-I, no blank. $30.00 – 45.00.

Plate 424. Siskin bird plate; .8h x 7.9d; D-621h; "Small Birds - Siskin"; TM-I, no blank. $30.00 – 45.00.

Plate 425. Weaver bird plate; 0.8h x 7.9d; D-621i; "Small Birds - Red Billed Weaver"; TM-I, no blank. $30.00 – 45.00.

165

Plate 426. Finch bird plate; 0.8h x 7.9d; D-621j; "Small Birds Dimond Finch"; TM-I, no blank. There is no "a" in the WDCO spelling of the word "Diamond." $30.00 – 45.00.

Plate 427. Gold finch plate; 0.8h x 8d; D-621a; "Small Birds - Gold Finch"; TM-I and TM-M, no blank, Homer Laughlin theme. $30.00 – 55.00.

Plate 428. Brown finch plate; 0.8h x 8d; D-621b; "Small Birds - Brown Finch"; TM-M, no blank, Homer Laughlin theme. $30.00 – 55.00.

Plate 429. Baltimore Oriole plate; 0.8h x 8d; D-621c; "Small Birds - Baltimore Oriole"; TM-I & TM-M, no blank, Homer Laughlin theme. $30.00 – 55.00.

Plate 430. Bul Bul glass; 5.6h x 2.7d; D-621k; "Small Birds - Bul Bul"; no trade-mark, no blank. $25.00 – 40.00.

Plate 431. Weaver water glass; 6.1h x 3d; D-621i; "Small Birds - Red Billed Weaver"; no trade-mark, no blank. $25.00 – 40.00.

Plate 432. Finch bourbon glasses; 3.3h x 3d; D621j; "Small Birds - Dimond Finch"; no trademark, no blank. Different artist painting the same bird. $25.00 – 40.00 each.

Plate 433. Trophy glass with mallard; 3.8h x 2.7w; D-622a; "Raised Birds - Flying Mallard"; no trademark, no blank. $70.00 – 100.00.

Plate 434. Bird glasses; 3.6h x 2.8d; D-621b, D621l, D621f; "Small Birds - Brown Finch, Cardinal, Robin"; no trademark, no blank. Not U.S. cardinal. $25.00 – 40.00 each.

Plate 435. Liqueur glass; 4h x 1.7d; D-622b; "Raised Birds - Ringed Necked Pheasant"; no trademark, no blank. $65.00 – 85.00.

Plate 436. Tall bird glasses; 7.6h x 2.7d; D-622e, i, b, a, j, f; "Raised Birds - Various"; no trademark, no blank; scarce. $25.00 – 45.00 each.

Plate 437. Thick rimmed shot glasses; 2.5h x 2.2d; D-622a; "Raised Birds - Flying Mallard"; no trademark, no blank. $35.00 – 55.00 each.

Plate 438. Medium and thin rimmed shot glasses; 2.3h x 1.9d, 2.1h x 1.7d; D-622a; "Raised Birds - Flying Mallard"; no blank. $35.00 – 55.00, $30.00 – 50.00.

Plate 439. Mallard bitters bottle; 5.5h x 2.4sq; D-622a; "Raised Birds - Flying Mallard"; no trademark, no blank. Pour spout may not be original to bottle. $90.00 – 145.00.

Plate 440. Mallard cigarette box; 2.4h x 4.7l x 3.6w; D-622a; "Raised Birds - Mallard"; no trademark, no blank. $65.00 – 110.00.

Plate 441. Mallard ashtray; 1.6h x 8sq; D-622a; "Raised Birds - Mallard"; no trademark, no blank. $50.00 – 80.00.

Plate 442. Pheasant ashtray; 1.6h x 8sq; D-622b; "Raised Birds - Ring Necked Pheasant"; no trademark, no blank. $50.00 – 80.00.

Plate 443. Oval mallard ashtray; 1.5h x 7l x 4.5w; D-622a; "Raised Birds - Mallard"; no trademark, no blank. $55.00 – 85.00.

Plate 444. Small ashtrays; 0.8h x 3.6l x 2.6w, 1.1h x 4.9l x 3.4w, 0.9h x 3.4sq; D-622b, D-622a, D-622b; "Raised Birds, a) Mallard, b) and c) Ring Necked Pheasant"; no trademark, no blank. $40.00 – 70.00 each.

Plate 447. Three green bar ware glasses; 6.5h x 3.1d; D-623b, D-623c, D-623d; "Sweet Ad-Aline"; no trademark, no blank, probably Dunbar Glass. $20.00 – 35.00 each.

Plate 446. Green bar ware shaker; 11h x 4d; D-623a; "Sweet Ad-Aline - Drunks Singing"; no trademark, no blank, probably Dunbar Glass. We have heard that Dunbar Glass advertised bar ware in the *New Yorker* magazine in October, November, and December of 1931. $75.00 – 120.00.

Plate 448. Three green bar ware glasses; 6.5h x 3.1d; D-623e, D-623a, D-623f; "Sweet Ad-Aline"; no trademark, no blank, probably Dunbar Glass. $20.00 – 35.00 each.

Plate 449. Three small green bar ware glasses; 3.9h x 2.3d; D-623a, D-623d, D-623e; "Sweet Ad-Aline - Various"; no trademark, no blank, probably Dunbar Glass. $20.00 – 30.00 each.

Plate 450. Three small green bar ware glasses; 3.9h x 2.3d; D-623b, D-623c, D-623f; "Sweet Ad-Aline, Various"; no trademark, no blank, probably Dunbar Glass. $20.00 – 30.00 each.

Plate 451. Decorative fruit plate; 1.1h x 7.7d; D-624a; "Fruit Plates - Apples and Grapes"; TM-J, no blank. Transfer center design for this series. $75.00 – 110.00.

Plate 452. Pink bar ware glass; 6.5h x 3.1d; D-623a; "Sweet Ad-Aline - Drunks Singing"; no trademark, no blank, probably Dunbar Glass. Less common than the green Sweet Ad-Aline items. $30.00 – 45.00.

Plate 453. Decorative fruit plate; 1.1h x 7.7d; D-624b; "Fruit Plates - Plums and Raspberries"; TM-J, no blank. Center transfer pattern. $75.00 – 110.00.

Plate 454. Decorative fruit plate; 1.1h x 7.7d; D-624c; "Fruit Plates - Strawberries and Blackberries"; TM-J, no blank. Transfer center. $75.00 – 110.00.

Plate 455. Decorative fruit plate; 1.1h x 7.7d; D-624d; "Fruit Plates - Pears and Grapes"; TM-J, no blank. Center is a transfer pattern. $75.00 – 110.00.

Plate 456. Golf ashtray; 0.9h x 6d; D-625a; "Golf Related Items - Two Clubs and Golf Ball"; TM-J, no blank; scarce. $20.00 – 35.00.

Plate 457. Golf pitcher; 9h x 3.7d; D-625a; "Golf Related Items - Two Clubs and a Golf Ball"; no trademark, no blank. $80.00 – 125.00.

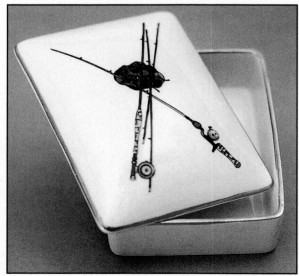

Plate 458. Cigarette box; 2.7h x 5.3l x 4.1w; D-626a; "Fishing Related Items - Four Poles and a Hat"; TM-J, no blank. $25.00 – 35.00.

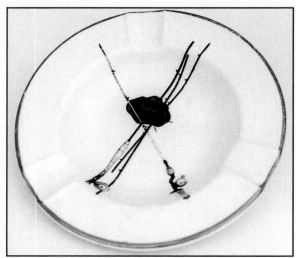

Plate 459. Fishing ash tray; 5.8h x 4d; D-626a; "Sports Related Items - Four Poles and a Hat"; TM-J, no blank. $10.00 – 20.00.

Plate 460. Fruit bowl; 4.1h x 5.9d; D-627a; "Royal Guardsmen Series - Life Guard"; no trademark, no blank; scarce. WDCO did a series from Schenley Whiskey ads. This is thought to be part of it. $75.00 – 95.00.

Plate 461. Man O' War plate; 1.1h x 10d; D-628a; "Animal Related Items - Man O' War"; TM-M, no blank, Homer Laughlin theme. $25.00 – 45.00.

Plate 462. Retriever display plate; 1.1h x 10.5d; D-628b; "Animal Related Items - Retriever with Duck"; TM-J, no blank. $20.00 – 30.00.

Plate 463. Horse plate; 1.1h x 8d; D-628c; "Animal Related Items - Horse Head with Double Bridle"; TM-M, no blank, Homer Laughlin theme. $25.00 – 50.00.

Plate 464. Horse head glasses; 5.7h x 2.7d, 5.9h x 2.9d; D-628c, D-628d; "Animal Related Items - c) Horse head with Double Bridle, d) Horse head with Single Bridle"; no trademark, no blank. $20.00 – 35.00 each.

Plate 465. Golden rooster stem; 5.3h x 2.8d; D-630a; "Rooster - Golden Rooster"; no trademark, no blank, rare. $40.00 – 60.00.

Plate 466. Martini glass; 5.6h x 2.9d; D-630b; "Rooster - Multicolored Rooster - Wing Back"; no trademark, no blank; rare availability. $45.00 – 65.00.

Plate 467. Rooster martini glass; 5.6h x 2.9d; D-630c; "Rooster - Multicolored Rooster, Wing Down"; no trademark, no blank, rare availability. $45.00 – 65.00.

Plate 468. Christmas ashtray; 0.9h x 5.1d; D-650; "Christmas Tree and Toys"; TM-J, no blank. $15.00 – 25.00.

Plate 469. Clematis vase; 7.5h x 6l x 2.8w; D-652; "Clematis Flowers"; TM-h, no blank. Rare, painted on both sides. $110.00 – 150.00.

Plate 470. Decal or veined leaf plate; 1h x 7.2d; D-651; "Poppy and Birds"; TM-J, no blank, Made in Japan. Similar veined leaf plate in Plate 121. $30.00 – 50.00.

Plate 471. Design enlargement; D-653l; "Mythical Beast and Flowers"; rare availability. Design on engraving plate tracing.

Plate 472. Design enlargement; D-653-II; "Mythical Beast and Flowers"; rare availability.

Plate 473. Candy jar; 9.2h x 4d; D-653; "Mythical Beast"; no trademark, no blank, Heisey. $140.00 – 200.00.

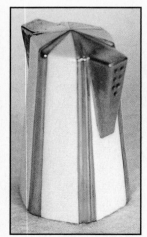

Plate 474. Salt and pepper combo; 3.5h x 2.3l x 2.1w; D-654; "Lenox Dual Salt and Pepper"; TM-K, no blank, Lenox; scarce availability. $25.00 – 45.00.

Plate 475. Design enlargement; D-655; "Three Leaf Pattern"; plentiful availability. From photographed and collected items. D-655 items are only known on Libby glassware. They called this pattern "Gold Leaves." WDCO may have been contracted by Libby to make these glasses.

Plate 476. Gold and silver bourbon glasses; 4h x 3.1d, 3.5h x 2.7d; D-655; "Three Leaf Pattern"; no trademark, no blank. Libby. Silver is uncommon. $5.00 – 8.00, $12.00 – 15.00.

Plate 477. Three leaf water glass; 4.7h x 2.9d; D-655; "Three Leaf Pattern"; no trademark, no blank. Libby. $6.00 – 9.00.

Plate 478. Three leaf items; 5h x 2.8d, 4.6h x 3.2d; D-655; "Three Leaf Pattern"; no trademark, no blank. Libby. $5.00 – 8.00 each.

Plate 479. Three leaf sherbets; 4.3h x 3.5d, 4.7h x 3.6d; D-655; "Three Leaf Pattern"; no trademark, no blank. Libby. $5.00 – 8.00 each.

Plate 480. Design enlargement; D-656; "Rose and Buds"; infrequent availability. From photographed and collected items. D-656 items are only known on Libby glassware.

Plate 481. Rose sherbet and water glass; 3.8h x 2.9d, 5.4h x 3.3d; D-656; "Rose and Birds"; no trademark, no blank. Libby. $6.00 – 10.00 each.

Plate 482. Whiskey shaker; 6.9h x 2.9d; D-657; "Rider and Fox Hunt"; no trademark, no blank. $110.00 – 155.00.

Plate 483. Fox hunt glasses; 3.6h x 2.8d, 6.1h x 3.1d, D-658; "Two Riders and Fox Hunt"; no trademark, no blank. Other hunt scenes included D-657, D-58, D-82, and D-220. D-658 scene is found on etch plate copy. Each glass, $40.00 – 50.00.

Plate 484. Machine-cut ruby stem; 5h x 4d; D-659; "Machine Cut Duck"; no trademark, no blank; scarce availability. Item came from home of WDCO employee. $75.00 – 100.00.

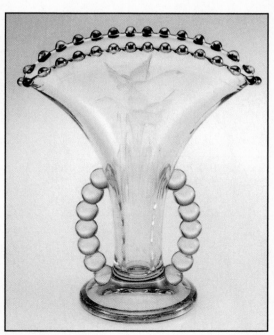

Plate 485. Machine cut fan vase; 8.5h x 7l x 3.5d; D-659; "Machine Cut Duck"; no trademark, no blank, Imperial Glass Company; scarce availability. $95.00 – 125.00.

Plate 486. Alcohol bottle; 5.2h x 2.4l x 2.4w; D-660; "Alcohol Bottle with Twin Stemmed Flowers"; no trademark, no blank. $80.00 – 125.00.

Plate 487. Flutist ashtray; 0.8h x 5.4d; D-661; "Flute Playing Nymph"; TM-J, no blank; scarce availability. $25.00 – 40.00.

Plate 488. Design enlargement; D-662; "Nine Petal Flowers and Open Vases"; scarce availability. Enclosed by ribbon-stamped fleur-de-lis type pattern and D-46a.

Plate 489. Charger with transfer flowers; 1h x 10.8d; D-662; "Nine Petal Flowers and Open Vases"; TM-H, no blank. $70.00 – 95.00.

Plate 490. Round rose vase; 4.8h x 5d; D-663; "Gold Roses on White"; TM-J, no blank, Andover China Company. $65.00 – 90.00.

Plate 491. Cream and sugar; 3h x 3.6d, 2.6h x 3.6d; D-663; "Gold Roses on White"; TM-I, no blank; scarce availability. $35.00 – 55.00 per set. Cream, sugar, and pitcher set valued at $120.00 – 160.00.

Plate 492. Design enlargement; D-664; "Interlocking Arrow Points with Three Swags"; rare availability. Has D-46a as an inside border. Laurel leaves are D-3c. Similar to D-46.

Plate 493. Charger; 1h x 10.7d; D-664; "Interlocking Arrow Points with Three Swags and Laurel Leaves"; no trademark, no blank, Royal Bavarian Hutschenreuther. $175.00 – 225.00.

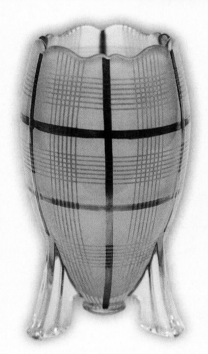

Plate 494. Rocket vase with plaid design; 8.3h x 4.7d; D-900; singular item. Belonged to Lee Taylor's wife.

Plate 495. Juice glasses; 3.7h x 2d; D-900; "Singular Items." Were with D-256 juice glass but may be one-of-a-kind test. Pattern on the left is shown on an etch plate copy.

Plate 497. Gold banded vase; 5.2h x 4.3d; D-900; singular item. Belonged to Leland Taylor's wife.

Plate 496. Bud vase; 10.1h x 2.9d, 6.2h x 1.9d; D-900; "Singular Items - Golden Roses on Pink Vase, Gold Banded Vase"; no trademark, no blank.

Plate 498. Fan-shaped flower vase; 4.9h x 7.4w; D-900; singular item; no trademark, no blank. Have seen the same vase in AOG D-11. $65.00 – 105.00.

Plate 499. Mallard tray; 22l x 12w; D-900; singular item; no trademark, no blank. Decorated by WDCO artist.

Chapter 6: *Design Pattern Numbers and Names*

Very few of the WDCO design names come from the Design Book itself. We created most of the names and tried to choose titles that would help people remember which pattern was being discussed. We have tried to make the design names descriptive of some part of the design pattern. The designs are given a design "D" letter, followed by the Design number. Thus, the D-11 design is the "Doves, Roses, and Daisies" pattern, which is the most common all-over-gold (AOG) pattern as well as the most common WDCO pattern. The D-1 pattern, listed below, has never been found on any china or glassware item so it is not shown in the photographic section. Most patterns that have not been found in production pieces are not even listed. Still, we feel confident that eventually, most design patterns will be found.

Design Number	Descriptive Name
1	Minton No. I – Leaf and Flower Swag (not shown).
2a	Minton No. IIa – Fingered Swirls , Arrows, and Flowers.
2b	Minton No. IIb – Hammer Ending Fingered Swirls, Arrows, and Flowers.
3	Laurel Leaves with Multiple Dots (can be from six to 10 dots, except as noted below). (See Plate 7.)
3a	Laurel Leaves with Single Dot (not shown).
3b	Laurel Leaves with Four Dots.
3c	Laurel Leaves with Two to Five Dots (see border on Plate 214).
6	Hobart Etching – "Diamond Connected 'M's' or 'W's'."
7	Roses and Thorns.
8	Three Leaf Clover (see border on Plate 312).
10	Rambler Rose – The WDCO may be unique in that at the end of every other vine there is a ball-shaped fruit. Most other decorators used a balled fruit at the end of each hanging vine.
11	Doves, Roses, and Daisies. The Pickard "Rose and Daisy" pattern is similar to this Dove pattern, but the Dove pattern was introduced several years before the Pickard pattern. This is the most common WDCO pattern for AOG. It is called "Love Birds" by some.
12	Aligned Periwinkles.
13	Leaf Twisted Rope.
14	Headdress. This design is often copied. (Pattern D-76 is similar.)
16	Leaf Formed Arrowhead Border.
25	Running Vine Border.
30	Flowers and Ferns on Platters.

Design Number	Descriptive Name
31	Stylized Eight-Petal Flowers Separated by Diamonds.
33	Stacked Ovals with Inside Diamonds.
34	Anhingas and Urns.
35	Up and Down Connected Arrow Points.
36	Circles with Plus Signs (see D-68, Plate 280, for this border pattern).
38	Coreopsis, Ferns, and Arbors.
42	Flower and Fern-Filled Basket.
46	Swags, Laurel Leaves, and Tulips.
46a	Tulip Border.
47	Maple Leaf and Beads (wide border). (D-99 is similar but not shown).
47a	Maple Leaf and Beads (with interior doily).
51	Drapes.
53	Pheasant and Stump.
56	Fruit Urns with Squared Borders.
57	Fox and Hounds. (D-58e means etched. D-82 and D-220 are similar but not shown.)
61	Encircled Twelve-Petaled Flowers with Dot-Dash Border.
63	Butterfly-Like Flowers and Falling Ferns.
65	Honeysuckle Swag with Grill Windows. (D-121 is similar but not shown).
67	Short flowered Urns with Multi-flowered Panels.
68	Checker Flags and Sprays.
74	Nymphs Holding Garlands.
75	Three Birds on Hanging Vine.
76	Headdress II. (Similar to D-14 but fewer radial circles near round flower.)
77	Aztec Triangles Five.
90	Border of Semi-circles and Arrow Points.
90a	Mixed Flowers, Fruit, and Leaves.
90b	Rose Buds and Ten-Petal Flower.
90c	Leafed Plumes with Windows.

Design Number	Descriptive Name
90d	Alyssums.
90e	Doubled Leafed Plumes with Windows.
92	Scrolls with Kites and Dangling Flowers.
97	Etched Poinsettias, Panel and Coral Bell Border.
100a	Swinging Nymphs and Potted Plants. (Enclosed by D-6.)
100b	Swinging Nymphs and Potted Plants. (Enclosed by D-8.)
101	Greek Key Border.
101a	Encircled Flower Basket.
102	Latticed Vines.
125a	Double Connected Roses.
125b	Double Connected Flowers.
127	Large Gold Daisy and Silver Urn.
133	Draped Covered Urn with Flowers.
137	Wreath-Enclosed Flower with Shark Tooth Border.
153	Impatiens with Squiggles.
169	Twigs, Leaves, and Roses.
204c	Griffins Smelling Flowers.
204g	Hanging Garland and Shields.
256	A Single Orange.
298	Sixes or Nines with Flowers. (The "6" or "9" border alone is D-313, not shown.)
301	Red and Black Laughing Fish.
320d	Meissen Flowers.

The numbers below represent specific items from steel etch plate copies, loose items in the WDCO Design Book, and other sources such as magazines and collections. The items listed within a category are those which we own or have photographed and are not necessarily those which we have observed on the Internet.

486	Game Birds. a) Mallard, b) Canada Goose, c) Bob White, d) Red Headed Duck, e) Blue Goose, f) Ring Necked Pheasant, g) Pintail Duck, h) Mountain Quail, i) Ruffed Grouse, j) Wild Turkey, k) Sage Hen, l) Prairie Chicken, (The rest of these were on an etch plate and have not yet been found. The I and II numbering shows there were two different forms of the bird shown). m) Canvas Back I, n) Canvas Back II, o) Snipe, p) American Merganser, q) California Quail, r) Blue Wing Teal, s) Black Duck I, t) Black Duck II, u) Mallard II.

Design Number	Descriptive Name
600	Pictorial Church Items. a) North Broadway Methodist, b) Dillon Chapel Methodist, c) Broad Street Methodist, d) Washington Cathedral, e) Franklin Street Methodist, f) Gatonsville United Methodist, g) Trinity Methodist, h) St. Stephen's Evangelical.
602	School Related Items. a) Barboursville High School, b) Cornell University.
604	Pictorial State Items. a) Oklahoma, b) Mississippi, c) Kentucky, d) Virginia, e) West Virginia, f) Pennsylvania.
606	Pictorial Family Items. a) Unknown home – two-story, white fronted house.
608	Pictorial Historical Items. a) Twin Tunnels – Pennsylvania Turnpike.
610	Organizational Items. a) Maritime Association.
612	Event Celebrations. a) Schaefer Beer, 1952.
618	Typical Floral Transfer Patterns for Plates. (Most of these transfers are not shown or named. The D-624 designs are all transfers). a) Mixed florals with Large Rose (see Plates 220 and 221), b) Large, Single Rose (Plate 196), c) Three Poppies with Daisies (see Plates 303 and 489).
621	Small Birds. a) Gold Finch, b) Brown Finch, c) Baltimore Oriole, d) Red Cardinal, e) Blue Grosbeak, f) Robin, g) Java SP., h) Siskin, i) Red Billed Weaver, j) Dimond Finch, k) Bul Bul, l) Cardinal. (Since most of these birds are foreign to North America, expected names may not apply.)
622	Raised Birds. a) Flying Mallard, b) Ring Necked Pheasant, c) Mountain Quail, d) Ruffed Grouse (with fanned tail), e) Swimming Mallard, f) Female Mallard With Wings Up, g) California Quail, h) Long-Billed Dowitcher, I) Prairie Chicken, j) Female Mallard, One Wing Down.
623	Sweet Ad-Aline. a) Singing Drunks with "Sweet Ad-Aline" Overhead, b) Drunk with Arm Around Lamp Post, c) Drunk Leaning on Lamp Post, d) Drunk Drinking from Bottle, e) Two Drunks Leaning on Lamp Post, f) Cop Looking at Bottle.
624	Fruit Plates. a) Apples and Grapes, b) Plums and Raspberries, c) Strawberries and Blackberries, d) Pears and Grapes.
625	Golf Related Items. a) Two Clubs and a Golf Ball.
626	Fishing Related Items. a) Four Poles and a Hat.

Design Number	Descriptive Name

627......................Royal Guardsman Series.
a) Life Guard.

628......................Animal Related Items.
a) Man O' War, b) Retriever with Duck, c) Horse Head with Double Bridle, d) Horse Head with Single Bridle.

630......................Roosters.
a) Golden Rooster, b) Multicolored Rooster, Wing Back, c) Multicolored Rooster, Wing Down.

Below are several isolated items that were not placed in other categories.

650......................Christmas Tree and Toys.

651......................Poppy and Buds.

652......................Clematis Flowers.

653......................Mythical Beast and Flowers – From Engraving Plate.

654......................Lenox Dual Salt and Pepper.

655......................Three Leaf Pattern – From Photographs and Collected Items called "Gold Leaves" on Libby Glass box.

656......................Rose and Buds – From Photographs and Collected Items.

657......................Rider and Fox Hunt.

658......................Two Riders and Fox Hunt.

659......................Machine Cut Duck.

660......................Alcohol Bottle with Twin Stemmed Flowers.

661......................Flute Playing Nymph.

662......................Nine-Petal Flowers and Open Vases.

663......................Gold Roses on White – From Photographs and Collected Items.

664......................Interlocking Arrow Points with Three Swags.

Singular items, thought to have been made by WDCO artisans, will be listed in a D-900 category (Singular) until it can be shown that they were produced in some significant quantity. Though pictures of some of these items will be shown, no listing names or prices will be given.

900.......................Singular Items.

A wide variety of blanks were purchased from various manufacturers of china/pottery/glassware for use by the WDCO. To identify these sources, WDCO often put a handwritten gold number on the bottom of the item being decorated. This numbering system was not used on glassware, obviously, as this would detract from the beauty of the item. Only one exception is known to the hand numbering system. The number "359" is stamped on the back of some charger plates in square block letters. These chargers have a colored floral transfer center, a wide light gold on blue transfer band of flowers, and two etched bands of gold.

Some of the gold numbers show up more frequently than others. In the listing below the blank number is shown first, followed, in parentheses, by the number of times the blank number appears in the author's collection of about 500 pieces. (Many more of the WDCO numbers can be found in the various online auctions). If the manufacturer of the item is known, it is listed next. In a very few examples, a blank number is proceeded by a "K." The reason for this is not known, but the blank number associated with the "K" is from the same product line as a blank without the "K." We assume that the "K" number represents a small change in the previously numbered blank from that manufacturer. For several manufacturers, more than one number was used for that company. Often, a blank number was chosen to correspond with a number the manufacturer had already given to a particular item. An example of this is seen with the Hall China Company of East Liverpool, Ohio. The blank numbers 630, 631, and 641 all represent specific items made by Hall and decorated in all-over-gold patterns by WDCO. Most times, the Hall number was coated over by some form of gold so as to hide the Hall number and name. In general, the distribution of the numbers used and frequency of their use would make one think that closely related numbers may be for the same blank manufacturer.

There is at least one case where a half number was used. There is the gold number 236 and a gold number 236½ The leaf dish with the 236½ is a quarter of an inch larger in diameter than the one with the 236. Many times only a country of origin is shown along with the gold blank number, though any number of companies from within that country could have made the blank item. A number of WDCO items (mostly china and pottery) have no gold number on them, but do have a manufacturer's name or backstamp that allows for identification. And, as discussed in Chapter 2, the name "Ransom" is used on many of the Wheeling decorated items, but there is never a gold number on these items. Many collectors of a particular manufacturer will be able to look at a photograph of a WDCO item and make a proper connection as to what company belongs to a particular blank number.

Blank Number	Times Found	Manufacturer's Name	Blank Number	Times Found	Manufacturer's Name
2	(3)		174	(1)	
4	(3)		204	(2)	
5	(16)	Steubenville Pottery Co.	205	(1)	
K-5	(3)	Steubenville Pottery Co.	236	(1)	
6	(1)		236½	(1)	
10	(3)		237	(1)	
12	(2)		256	(1)	
13	(3)	Taylor, Smith, & Taylor – Lu Ray	312	(1)	Japan
14	(1)		335	(1)	
15	(7)		351	(3)	Trenton Potteries Co. (TAC)
18	(1)		359	(2)	
19	(1)		360	(2)	Hutschenreuther Selb
20	(1)		417	(2)	
28	(2)		418	(4)	
31	(1)		419	(2)	
76	(1)		420	(1)	
91	(2)		432	(1)	
103	(1)		509	(1)	
104	(3)		538	(2)	
155	(1)		598	(2)	

Blank Number	Times Found	Manufacturer's Name	Blank Number	Times Found	Manufacturer's Name
601	(1)		1256	(1)	
603	(1)		1260	(1)	
625	(4)		1553	(1)	
626	(9)	Homer Laughlin China Co.	1706	(1)	
627	(4)		1724	(1)	
630	(4)	Hall China Co.	1726	(3)	
631	(2)	Hall China Co.	1960	(4)	
637	(3)	Winterling, Bavaria	2154	(1)	
641	(1)	Hall China Co.	2264	(2)	
650	(2)	Arzberg 473 M.I., Germany	2317	(1)	
831	(1)	Czechoslovakia	2821	(2)	Hutschenreuther Selb
912	(1)	Schumann, Bavaria, Ger.	4529	(2)	
914	(1)		4624	(1)	
1037	(2)	Japan	5606	(1)	
1040	(1)		6218	(1)	Japan
1047	(1)		6228	(1)	
1049	(3)		6248	(1)	
1051	(1)		7001	(1)	Trenton Potteries Co. (TAC)
1105	(5)		7066	(1)	Japan
1196	(1)		7774	(1)	Japan
1202	(2)		9002	2)	Trenton Potteries Co. (TAC)
1204	(1)		9037	(1)	
1228	(1)		9216	(3)	
1253	(12)	Arzberg Porcelain, Bavaria	Ransom	(10)	Warwick and Hutschenreuther

There are a number of companies that have their trademarks on Wheeling decorated pieces but no gold number was applied to these particular items. Likewise, Internet auctions list many WDCO glassware items and also list who they think made these blanks. Below are listed a number of such firms from these two categories.

C. T. Altwasser, Germany
Cambridge Glass Company
Central Glass Works
Dunbar Glass Co.
Duncan & Miller Glass Co.
Royal Epiag, Czech.
Fenton Art Glass Co.
Fostoria Glass Co.

A.H. Heisey Glass Co.
Imperial Glass Co. (Candlewick)
Lenox China Co.
Limoges China Co.
Limoges, France
McKee
Morgantown Glass Works
Northwood Glass Co.

Paden City Glass Co.
Rosenthal
R. S. Germany
Racine PHR, Bavaria
Schkacken-Werth Antoinettel
Tiffin Glass Company
R. S. Tillowilz
U.S. Glass Company

Appendices

Appendix A

From the January 19, 1936, *Wheeling News-Register* of Wheeling, West Virginia

Decorating Company Observes 25th Anniversary

Frank H. Thurm brought secret of process from his native country.

Plant first established in old club house on National Road

Twenty-five years ago this month the first plate-etched glass in the United States was turned in the city of Wheeling at the Wheeling Decorating Company.

Frank H. Thurm, head of that company, as a young man had carried the secret of the process from his native Dresden, Germany, a great glass center. When Mr. Thurm got into the glass business here at the turn of the century, plate-etching was unknown. He was a young man without funds but with ambition and a definite idea. His first job was at the old Ohio Valley China Company which used to be on Fourth Street. This plant, which had been skidding for some time, went out of business in a short time. He was without a job but with some funds and still with that same idea that as a sales center for plate-etched glass, America was just a big fat oyster ready to be cracked.

So, with what funds he had Mr. Thurm surveyed the situation and the landscape. He saw an old club house, standing abandoned, at Mount Wood and National Road. "Just the place to get into business for myself," he remarked, and the thought was father to the act.

For four years at the "club house" Frank Thurm followed the orthodox American fashion of glass decorating which was to apply color by the mere application of a brush with some paint on the business end of it. For those four years, too, he kept visualizing that day when something new and different would be on the American market — yes, on American buffets, bars and tables — an innovation that would be taken up by concerns in many localities.

Established Present Plant

In 1904 Frank Thurm had become quite substantial and really started business in a rather large way when he and one of his early co-workers at the Ohio Valley China company, Robert Englehart, took over what was the old Kenny Brewery building at Market and Seventh Streets, the present site of the Wheeling Decorating Company, recognized everywhere as producers of some of the finest quality etched and otherwise decorated glassware in the United States.

All of which leads up to the story of a substantial Wheeling industry — not one of the largest by any means — which has gone right along through lean times and fat and which makes employment for up to as many as 80 Wheeling people.

But how is this interesting business carried on? Well,

something like this. If a glass plate is to be etched, the plain crude plate is taken up by a worker and the print of a steel "plate" is applied to the glass plate. Then the paper on which the impression has been taken is removed from the glass. The impression remains. Then the glass plate on which the impression has been made is given over to another department. Here it is entirely covered with a gum or wax solution, like paraffin — covered all over, that is, except on that part where the impression of the design has been made. Then it is placed into a solution of sulphuric and hydroflouric acid. The acid, coming in contact with the metal impression, literally "eats" that impression into the glass. Then it is placed into a furnace heated to 300 degrees Fahrenheit, and this heat completes the fusion of the metal in the glass, bringing about a perfect etching. Then it is polished down, packed and ready for shipment. In the case of an etching on chinaware, practically the same process is followed except that it is placed into another oven heated to 1200 degrees.

All encrusted gold work is etched and the gold applied immediately afterward.

Small Waste

Waste in the etching process is very small. Near the ovens at the plant can be seen a number of boxes of broken articles. It was explained that these articles are thrown into nitric acid, the gold is removed and used over again. Eight artists work to put on the finishing touches to highball glass, cocktail shakers, water goblets, martini and champagne glasses, liquor and wine, Tom and Jerry sets, console dishes, relish trays, candlesticks, candy boxes, and trays for relishes, cheese, and crackers. In the china line are the salt and pepper shakers, gold-encrusted bon-bons and sugar-and-creams, cake plates, tea cups and saucers and bowls.

In fact, in going through room after room of Wheeling Decorating's product, it is a fairyland of color.

At the recent glass show held in Pittsburgh, the products of Wheeling Decorating drew wide praise from critics and buyers from all parts of the country. Several glass manufacturing concerns in the Valley district had exhibits there, and it is from these concerns that Wheeling Decorating acquires much of the product which is decorated at the plant at Market and Seventh Streets.

Appendix B

Interview with Mr. Leland Taylor of the Wheeling Decorating Company
for the Panorama Program of Radio Station WWVA of Wheeling, West Virginia, May 1956

Interviewer: Mr. Taylor, I wager one person out of a hundred does not know what goes on here at Wheeling Decorating Company; it seems to me to be a most unusual industry and from the outlook of the place outside, it looks like you are trying to get by with something.

Mr. Taylor: No, we are not trying to get by with anything but I would say there isn't one out of a thousand knows this place is here in Wheeling, although it has been here for 55 years.

Interviewer: I had to walk about two miles to get here and now I am glad I am here, but I have seen and gone through your warehouse and you have been kind enough to go over the things you make. I wonder if you could explain to the listening audience just what you do here.

Mr. Taylor: Well, we decorate china and glassware. We do not make any china or glass; we buy all our blanks plain and just do the decorating, all hand decorated. Most of our china is imported from Germany and Japan. The glassware we buy from different factories in the valley, from Weston, Bellaire, and Moundsville, and different places in the valley, and we send it all over the country and we export some, not a whole lot.

Interviewer: You don't do too much business right here in Wheeling, do you?

Mr. Taylor: Very little here in Wheeling. The local department stores and jewelry stores don't patronize our home products very much.

Interviewer: Oh, I see. Let's say for example, you get a shipment of just plain blank plates, dinner plates, from Germany. What happens when they come to your plant?

Mr. Taylor: Well, it all depends what we want on them. If we do — a large percentage of our china with all over gold encrusted, of course, that goes through different processes, and it would start in the printing, what they call the printing room, the wax room, the acid room, the washing room, the decorating room and the polishing room.

Interviewer: I have seen the most exquisite art work on your glasses and plates. Do you have a staff of artists to do that?

Mr. Taylor: Well, the one artist that makes, for instance, our raised enamel game birds, assorted, started when he was 13 years old in Germany. He is now 76. As I told you, at the time, he was not able to write his own name

with a pencil but when he gets a brush in his hand he settles down and can raise these birds and decorates very nicely.

Interviewer: Truly remarkable. Of course, doing the work he does, he does not have to write his own name, does he?

Mr. Taylor: That's right. No, it isn't necessary.

Interviewer: I have looked over some of your glasses, all kinds of glasses, goblets, and what have you and they all seem to be marvelously done. Where do these glasses go?

Mr. Taylor: Well, they go to nearly all the better jewelry stores all over the United States. These goblets or stemware line — which are the goblet, sherbet and ice teas and different things to match.

Interviewer: Do you use real gold on these?

Mr. Taylor: Real gold and real palladium, a lot of palladium or platinum bands to match dinnerware patterns.

Interviewer: And you also get orders from, say, officers' clubs and universities?

Mr. Taylor: Yes. We had one order right after World War II we sent to the Philippine Islands for an officers' club.

Interviewer: With their insignia on the glass?

Mr. Taylor: That's right, with their insignia on the glass and the number of their company.

Interviewer: Do you get many unusual orders here?

Mr. Taylor: Yes, we get quite a few. Anything that anyone wants made up we can photograph; anything that is photographable we can photograph it and produce the exact same thing on glass. I take a college seal or golf club, anyone playing golf can take a photograph and reproduce that, and put that right on the glass.

Interviewer: What's been one of your most remarkable orders? Can you think back? Something you have been very proud of.

Mr. Taylor: Well, now just last year we photographed a man playing golf, in a golf club over in New Jersey, and it was given as a prize, and they had several dozen that

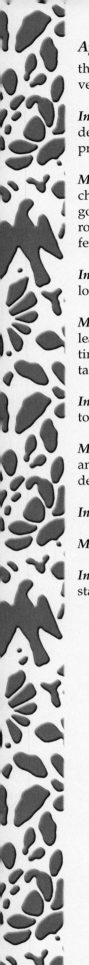

they gave out as prizes over there and this was very, very nice.

Interviewer: Now, in order to produce these wonderful designs on glass, it is necessary to go through several processes, isn't it?

Mr. Taylor: Yes, as I mentioned before, glass and the china both, it has to start in the printing room and it goes from the printing room to the acid room, the wax room and on through. It goes through six or eight different hands.

Interviewer: Mr. Taylor, it seems to me this is almost a lost art, is it?

Mr. Taylor: Yes, it is almost a lost art, no one wants to learn the trade any more, and the old fellows are getting too old and dying off and there is just no one to take it up.

Interviewer: They can make these things cheaply in factories, can't they, sir?

Mr. Taylor: Not hand decorated. They can make decals and silk screen work and things like that but not hand decorated work.

Interviewer: This is for the connoisseur?

Mr. Taylor: Yes.

Interviewer: Mr. Taylor, I wonder how this place got started. Can you tell me?

Mr. Taylor: Well, it started back in 1913 by Mr. Frank Thurm, and he was a decorator from Germany, and he and his partner at the time was Robert Englehart. They are both passed away now. Mr. Thurm was a watchman in the North Wheeling Pottery and he slept there and was given a little room, and in his spare time, he decorated and had a little kiln, and that's how he got started.

Interviewer: Would you be frank with Panorama listeners, are you having a good year, sir, or a bad year?

Mr. Taylor: It is not as good this year as it was last year; last year was a record year.

Interviewer: Really?

Mr. Taylor: That's correct, yes sir.

Interviewer: The art may be dying out but not the demand?

Mr. Taylor: Well, I have always found that the presidential election year is a little off in business, in nearly all businesses.

Interviewer: Mr. Taylor, it has been a pleasure talking to you and I want to say personally it has been a fascinating experience, and thanks for allowing me to come into your factory and talk to you on Panorama.

Mr. Taylor: Thank you very much for coming.

Appendix C
Undated Newspaper Article From About 1951

(Assumed to be from the *Wheeling News-Register*)
(The article is truncated and incomplete, as to other companies.)

"See Hand Painted Glass, Decorated China, Fluted Glasses, They are Valley Made"

It is natural that the Ohio Valley should become a center for decorated glass and clay products with a number of the countries largest glass companies and potteries in the area.

The old story, oft-told of the women who returned from San Francisco with the "darlingest" set of glasses — and reordered them consistently from the California city to find out eventually that they were made within five miles of her home, is repeated day after day in Wheeling.

Wheeling's largest decorating firm, The Wheeling Decorating Company, is deceptive in its appearance. Located on Market Street near 7th, the plant rambles back into the hill from a modest two-story brick building. Some of the neighbors, living within a half block of the plant, have no idea of its existence or of the products made there.

The Valley's decorating firms include the Wheeling Decorating, Decorative Clay Products in Warwood, The Lotus Glass Co. in Barnesville, The Belmont Tumbler Co. in Bellaire, The Porter Cut Class Co. in Martins Ferry, and the Sickles Cutting Shop in Bellaire.

Many of these decorating firms are specialists, performing only one type of operating. Others have a wide range of products.

The Wheeling Decorating Company, J. Leland Taylor, president; Walter Rupple, vice-president, and O. W. Crumley, secretary, is probably most noted for its gold-encrusted china and game bird glasses.

The business has been in operation for the past 51 years, being incorporated for the past two years. The production is difficult to state in a set amount per day — depending on the item being made that day, but an average of 60 dozen items go through the production process daily.

In a brief tour through the plant last week our scouts found many dozen of the gold encrusted china going through the production line, game bird glasses being produced; an order of bar goods, with the springhouse of White Sulphur Springs as an emblem being produced for the Greenbrier hotel; dozens of different college seals being affixed to drinking glasses; gold encrusted service plates and personalized beer mugs being made.

The game bird glasses are produced in two types -- flat full colored pictures, and built-up three dimensional birds on the glasses. Special enamel, imported from Europe, is used for the built-up birds.

Chances are that decorated drinking glasses you see advertised in the national magazines are produced right in Wheeling.

With sales offices in New York, Chicago, Durham, North Carolina, San Francisco, and Wabasso, Minnesota, the Wheeling Decorating Co. products may be retailed by outlets anywhere in the nation.

The raw materials, i.e., undecorated plates and glassware, come from many of the Valley producers and also from other sources in the United States and in Europe.

Presently there are 40 people employed by the Wheeling Decorating...

Appendix D

Remembering the Wheeling Decorating Company

By E. J. Feinler of Menlo Park, California

I worked for Wheeling Decorating Company the summer of 1947. I was sixteen years old and this was my first paying job other than babysitting. In those days there were very few jobs for female teenagers without any experience except working as a waitress or clerking in a store. Those jobs paid about $10 a week. Women working in the factories made much higher salaries because the companies were usually unionized but one had to be 18 to get such a job and the work was hard.

I saw an ad in the paper for a china decorator for the Wheeling Decorating Company. I had no idea what china decorating entailed, or whether I could do it. China decorating sounded more interesting than clerking, so I put together a portfolio of my drawings and art projects and appeared on their doorstep answering the ad. I was very naïve, but eager to work, so screwed up my courage to give it a try. I remember that the three men I talked to were rather amused by my youth and approach and were a little skeptical. I did my best to "sell" my art talent to them and they finally decided to give me a chance — probably because of my chutzpah as much as anything. I was careful to tell them that I had to return to high school in the Fall, but somehow this information seemed to slip through the cracks.

I was so excited to have landed the job, I didn't even think to ask them how much it paid. It paid the princely sum of $18 per week, as I recall, and we received our pay in cash in little manila envelopes at the end of the week. We also punched in and out using a time clock.

The work area was divided into two sections - one section was where we painted the china and the other was a room full of big kilns or furnaces where the painted china was fired.

The room in which we worked was a large work room with very high windows on one side. There were no curtains or shades on the windows and no air conditioning, as I remember, and it was very bright and hot. The room had the feeling of a factory. There were rows of heavy wooden work tables spattered with paint, and perhaps 20 women working at them. There were no rugs or other coverings on the floor, and the whole room had a kind of gray appearance from dripped paint and dust and worn surfaces.

There were four of us working at my table. Two of the women were older and married and one girl was much younger, closer to my age. I regret I do not remember the names of any of these women. We

worked hard and didn't have a lot of time for socializing, but did exchange pleasantries every morning, and chatted over lunch. The younger woman was a bit of a cut-up and a little on the clumsy side. More about this later.

We were given brushes, a small tabletop potter's wheel, and a bottle of brown paint. We signed out the "greenware" which was white china embossed with a small all-over pattern. We also signed out the brown paint and turned it in every night. My first assignment was to paint sugar and cream sets. I carefully painted them with the brown paint and a small brush. The "brown paint" turned out to be 24 karat gold paint and even then was worth a small fortune. We were admonished frequently not to spill it or otherwise waste it. I do not believe that we painted the inside of the sugar and cream sets, but am not sure about that. My recollection was that we had to make an even edge around the top of each piece.

When we finished painting a piece, we put it aside to dry and then put it in a large wooden box. When the box was filled with pieces, two of us would carry it to the door of the kiln room. All the workers there were men who did nothing but deal with the furnaces. The furnaces were brick, I think, and glowed red when they were opened to put the painted "greenware" in. When the pieces came out, they were the beautiful gold color associated with Wheeling Gold China. Unfortunately, we rarely saw the finished product because it went to a different area, so our view of that beautiful china was china painted an ugly brown color.

There was only one man on the floor where we worked. He was a kindly old gentleman who sat at the table near the door where we all came in. He was of German descent and rarely spoke in English. He would nod and smile at each of us when we came in, but otherwise said little. He worked very hard. Sometimes the other men came in to talk to him; however, they always spoke German and none of us understood German so didn't pay much attention.

As workers often do, we took occasional pot-shots at the management and the conditions and laughed about this procedure or carped about that. As it turned out the kindly old gentleman was the owner of the company, and he paid very close attention to what each of us was doing, and no doubt understood perfectly what we were saying. I cannot remember his name, but do remember it began with a "T."

One day the worker who was the cut-up was carrying one of the wooden boxes full of painted china to the kiln room. She was holding the back of the box and someone else was carrying the front of the box. The boxes probably held about 25 or 30 pieces of painted china. She was fooling around and tripped and dropped her end of the box. All of the china went clattering to the floor and most of it broke into smithereens. It was then we learned that the kindly old gentleman was the boss. He fired her on the spot. I lived in mortal fear the rest of the summer that I would trip and break a box of china and bring the wrath of the owner down on my head.

After a few weeks of painting sugar and cream sets, I was "promoted" to painting gold lines on white vases. To do this I put the vase in the middle of the potter's wheel and spun it. I then touched a brush full of gold paint to the whirling piece to put a thin line of gold decoration around the fullest part of the vase. This was not easy to do. If you spun the wheel too hard the piece was apt to fly off. If it wasn't spinning fast enough or you did not hold your hand steady, the line would not meet and the whole piece would have to be thrown out. Another problem was getting just the right amount of gold paint on the brush. Too much and the line was not an even width or "blobbed" at the beginning. Too little and there wasn't enough paint to complete the line. I remember I was shaking out of fear of not doing it right, and the line did not meet on the first couple of pieces I tried. However, I finally got the hang of it, and got pretty good by the time I left.

There were several men who worked in separate offices. One was Walter Knoblich. [Book author's note: E. J. Feinler is unsure who this was. It could have been Karl Knoblich or, more likely, Walter Ruppel.] He made beautiful dinner plates that were works of art. There was a lighted show case with examples of the plates that Wheeling Decorating had made along one side of a hallway. Walter told me that the company had made plates for famous people, royalty, and I believe some might have been made for the White House at one time. (Perhaps someone could research this point.)

I was fascinated by the process by which these plates were made and by Walter's skill and talent in making them. Most of these plates were white or ivory in color with very wide highly decorated rims. Some had center decorations such as royal crests. Others had the crests or insignias worked into the rim decoration.

I only got to observe Walter doing his work and to ask questions in spare moments, so I may not have a clear or complete picture of the process. As I remember it went something like this. Walter and the other designers would develop the design for the plate. This was then turned into a paper stencil which was applied to the plate. I do not know how the stencil was applied to the plate; however, once it was applied it appeared on the plate as an intricate filigree design. Walter would then begin "building" the design. Many of the plates had raised embellishments such as dots, or emblems. He built these up with something that looked like plaster of paris, but was probably some kind of ceramic mix because it withstood firing. Over this he added color and finally filled in with gold.

It took incredible skill to do this work, and he was a master craftsman. I sneaked in whenever I could manage to look over his shoulder. He was a very friendly and courtly gentleman, and explained what he was doing when there was time. Sometimes he made glasses which had built up flying ducks or geese on them. These were painted in authentic colors and fired. My mother had a set of these glasses, and they lasted for years without the decoration coming off or chipping.

One day Walter and two or three other men called me into the front office. The owner was there too. They said they had selected me to be an apprentice to learn how to make the beautiful plates. I was really thrilled but also disappointed because by this time it was August and almost time for me to go back to school. I tried to talk them into letting me work part-time. However, the owner seemed surprised that I was going to be leaving and felt that time had been wasted training me only to have me leave, so they let me go right then and there.

So ended my first paying job and my career as a china decorator. Now looking back I learned a lot, and it was a pleasure to have worked for a company that was part of the Wheeling glass and china heritage. It was also my pleasure to have met Walter Knoblich and to have observed his incredible talent and artistry.

Appendix E

REST FROM LABOR

Frank Herman Thurm

March 5, 1869   **April 18, 1949**

Gone to rest from labor and relief from suffering, our good friend has joined that innumerable throng in the Better Land.

A true friend to all, he served with no thought of self, and even during his latest hospital experience he ever remained bright and cheerful. He will be missed by every one who knew him—missed for his genial manner and his honest opinions, missed by the workers whom he always led; missed by Rotary because to know him well was to love him.

Our loss is great, but our gain from his service is also great. And we can thank a kind Providence that we had him as long as we did. His life has been a blessing and the memory of his works, of his many kindly, considerate acts, all without show or ostentation, will remain with us throughout this district.

Frank Herman Thurm was born March 5, 1869 in Dresden, Germany. His childhood days were spent at home and after early education he went to Teplitz, Bohemia (now Czecho-slovakia) where he evidenced a desire to become an artist, and taking up the decorating of China, Glass, etc. To still further improve his opportunities he became associated with a famous exporting concern "The House of Wallis" in Vienna, Austria. This institution was known the world over as a decorating shop of the highest quality. The lure of the New Country came to him and beckoned as the land of opportunity. In 1893 at the age of twenty-four, accompanied by several young friends, he came to the United States and shortly thereafter settled in Wheeling. Finding employment here, after a brief period he embarked on an enterprise of his own—the old North Wheeling Glass House under the name of the Wheeling Decorating Company—later moved to Pike and National Road and in 1910 came to the present location at Seventh and Market Streets. Here he continued to decorate glass and china and soon extended his business the width of the nation with Sales Representatives in New York on the East and San Francisco on the West, and from Canada to the Gulf. Wherever quality goods were appreciated he found no difficulty in opening accounts.

Married on July 23, 1903 to Miss Carrie Kalbitzer, his affectionate companion and helper, whom he leaves to mourn his passing.

A member of the Zion Lutheran Church—a Trustee of the congregation, fraternally a member in all the Masonic Bodies—Blue Lodge, Scottish Rite, Guards, Shrine, etc.—active in Y. M. C. A. and boys work in the hospitals—in fact all civic and cultural endeavors; active in the Arion Society. Joined Wheeling Rotary Decembber 1, 1925 and daily lived the life of service.

Rotary with friends throughout the district join in sympathy to the bereaved widow, and sorrowing relatives and friends.

Rotary obituray of Frank Herman Thurm, *The Lubricator,* Tuesday, April 26, 1949.

Appendix F

James Leland Taylor
March 30, 1900
May 23, 1957

Lee Taylor, quiet, unassuming, Christian gentleman has gone from amongst us. Long will he be remembered; sadly will he be missed.

Born March 30, 1900 in Hendrysburg, Ohio. He was a graduate of his local high school after which he attended and was graduated from the Elliott School of Business.

When he had finished at Elliott he joined the Wheeling Decorating Company where he climbed the ladder of success to the position of President and General Manager, which post he held at the time of his death.

He married Virginia Grosscurth, who survives, in 1924 and to this union were born Virginia Lee (now Mrs. James Nolan), Marietta (now Mrs. Raymond Norman) and James, Jr., who has just finished his third year at West Virginia University.

He was a Past Master of Ohio Lodge, Ancient, Free and Accepted Masons and a member of Wheeling Union Chapter, Royal Arch Masons. He was a member of Christ Methodist Church and had been a member of Rotary since September 20, 1949.

Lee Taylor was a devoted husband and father. He, together with his wife, liked to work with flowers in his summer home in the country. But his real hobby was his work at the plant.

Early and late through all the years he gave a full measure of devotion to his family, his job, his church, his lodge and his Rotary.

Staunch and true; upright and faithful—that was James Leland Taylor.

To his family and to all who mourn his passing we of Wheeling Rotary extend our deepest sympathy.

G. D. S.

Rotary obituray of James Leland Taylor, *The Lubricator,* Tuesday, June 25, 1957.

Appendix G

ALL SALES AND CONTRACTS ARE SUBJECT TO STRIKES, ACCIDENTS, FIRES OR OTHER UNAVOIDABLE DELAYS
ALL QUOTATIONS AND PRICES SUBJECT TO CHANGE WITHOUT NOTICE. ALL ORDERS SUBJECT TO FACTORY ACCEPTANCE.

MOSAIC ART GLASS CO.
DECORATED GLASS & CHINA
HUNTINGTON, W. VA
U.S.A.

OCTOBER 21, 1932.

MR. KARL KNOBLICH,
2201 HAZLETT AVE.,
WARWOOD,
WHEELING, W. VA.

MY DEAR MR. KNOBLICH:

SOMETIME AGO I HAD THE PLEASURE OF MEETING MR. RICHARD OTTO FOR THE FIRST TIME, AND AT THIS MEETING YOUR NAME WAS MENTIONED.

YOU, OF COURSE, REMEMBER MR. OTTO JAEGER WHO WAS IN THE DECORATING BUSINESS IN WHEELING FOR YEARS, THEN LATER MOVED TO HUNTINGTON AND OPERATED THE BONITA PLANT. IN 1929 MR. JAEGER'S PLANT WAS THROWN INTO BANK-RUPTCY. HOWEVER, IF A BUSINESS MAN WOULD HAVE BEEN CONNECTED WITH HIM THIS WOULD NOT HAVE HAPPENED. FOR YOUR INFORMATION, MR. JAEGER HAD OVER $50,000.00 OF MERCHANDISE ON HAND AND OWED LESS THAN $10,000.00. SO YOU CAN SEE WHY I SAY THAT THERE WAS NO OCCASION FOR THE BANKRUPTCY.

AFTER THE BANKRUPTCY, A NEW OUTFIT BOUGHT THE PLANT AND OPERATED IT AS THE BONITA GLASS CORPORATION. THESE PEOPLE, LIKE MYSELF, KNEW NOTHING ABOUT THE BUSINESS WITH THE RESULT THAT THEY LASTED LESS THAN TWO YEARS. I MIGHT ADD IN THIS CONNECTION THAT NOT ALONE DID THEY KNOW NOTHING ABOUT THE DECORATING BUSINESS, BUT AT THE SAME TIME THEY WERE NOT BUSINESS MEN.

ON AUGUST IST, OF THIS YEAR, I BOUGHT THEIR THE PLANT (NOT THE BUILDING), AND ALL OF THE TOOLS, EQUIPMENT, ETC. MR. JAEGER, AS YOU KNOW, IS GETTING UP IN YEARS, AND I AM ANXIOUS TO SECURE SOMEONE WHO HAS A THOROUGH KNOWLEDGE OF THE BUSINESS TO GO IN WITH ME IN THIS PLANT.

I WOULD LIKE FOR YOU TO SERIOUSLY CONSIDER A PROPOSITION OF JOINING ME IN THIS BUSINESS. I KNOW NOTHING ABOUT THE BUSINESS, BUT THE BUSINESS END OF IT I CAN HANDLE. IF YOU WILL COME TO HUNTINGTON, WHICH YOU CAN DO BY LEAVING WHEELING SOME SATURDAY NIGHT, ARRIVING HERE SUNDAY MORNING AND LEAVING HERE SUNDAY NIGHT, YOU CAN BE BACK IN WHEELING MONDAY MORNING. YOU WILL NOT LOSE ANY TIME, AND I BELIEVE THAT IF YOU WANT TO BECOME INTERESTED

Karl Knoblich Job Offer.

MOSAIC ART GLASS CO.

DECORATED GLASS & CHINA

HUNTINGTON, W. VA
U.S.A.

October 21, 1932.

MR. KARL KNOBLICH,   PAGE 2

IN A BUSINESS FOR YOURSELF THIS IS THE OPPORTUNITY THAT YOU HAVE BEEN LOOKING FOR. I DO NOT WANT ANY OF YOUR MONEY. I WANT YOUR KNOWLEDGE AND ABILITY TO MANAGE THE BUSINESS FROM THE PRODUCTION STANDPOINT, AND I WILL MAKE YOU A PROPOSITION THAT I DO NOT BELIEVE YOU CAN AFFORD TO TURN DOWN. IF IT IS NOT CONVENIENT FOR YOU TO COME DOWN AND SPEND SUNDAY WITH ME GOING OVER THE PLANT, THEN ANY OTHER TIME THAT YOU SUGGEST. WON'T YOU PLEASE LET ME HEAR FROM YOU, AND ADVISE ME WHEN YOU CAN MAKE IT CONVENIENT TO COME DOWN AND GO OVER THIS PROPOSITION WITH ME.

VERY TRULY YOURS,

S. J. HYMAN

SJH/H

Karl Knoblich Job Offer.

Excerpts from 1922 Warwick China "Ranson" line

Avon Shape — dinner Ware

THIS is the book of Warwick--the super-service china. Book of the AVON shape, which reproduces faithfully for the first time in American china, the popular imported design known as "Ranson".

Duplicates it in tough, vitrified china. How this china differs from most dinner ware made in America, this book tells.

Thousands of housewives possessing broken sets of French china in this design can fill in with "Avon". For the French china, besides being much more fragile than "Avon" is more expensive.

Dealer's Opportunity

Let the pictures in this book speak their own message. As you look at them, keep in mind, first, the high quality of Warwick china. Second, that there is a very large demand for the famous "Ranson" design. Third, that the "AVON" shape is the correct copy of the

original "Ranson" and is now offered for the first time in American china. It can be used to fill out depleted sets of this celebrated French design.

It is equally beautiful. It is a great deal more durable. It is much more economical.

In both shape and decoration we have duplicated the imported ware, thus creating a real opportunity for dealers.

Summary

Warwick china is vitrified. It is fired both before and after glazing.

AVON is our own name for the "Ranson" shape, of which it is a faithful reproduction produced in tougher material.

AVON can be used to fill out depleted sets of "Ranson", and will be found equally beautiful, doubly durable and much more economical.

Cream No.1

Sugar No.1

Fruit 4" 4½"

Tea Pot No.1

Celery

Pickel

Individual Salt

Cake

CoupeSoup 6"

Oatmeal

Dishes 8"–14"

Bibliography

1) Pickvet, Mark, *Official Price Guide to Glassware, Third Edition*, New York: The Ballantine Publishing Group, 2000.

2) Felt, Thomas G., *A. H. Heisey & Company, A Brief History*, published by Heisey Collectors of America, Inc., Newark, OH.

3) Reed, Alan B., *Collector's Encyclopedia of Pickard China*, Paducah, KY: Collector Books, 1995.

4) *Crockery and Glass Journal*, published G. Whittemore, NY, (1874-1961), weekly till 1928, then monthly.

5) Lehner, Lois, *Lehner's Encyclopedia of U. S. Marks on Pottery, Porcelain, & Clay*, Paducah, KY, Collector Books, 1988.

About The Author

Jim Webster, born in 1935, grew up in the north central portion of Oklahoma in the university town of Stillwater. His father, a knowledgeable and avid collector of American pottery, was a researcher and professor at Oklahoma State University. Jim went to school at OSU and graduated with a BS and PhD in Chemical Engineering. Dr. Webster  was also a Distinguished Military Graduate and stayed in the Reserves as a Captain for ten years. Upon graduation from OSU, Dr. Webster went to work for DuPont Chemical Company in 1966, first in Orange, Texas, then in Wilmington, Delaware, and he completed his 32-year DuPont career in Parkersburg, West Virginia. Much of his DuPont career was spent in various research organizations. He was also actively involved in the local and state activities of the United Methodist Church. Jim and his first wife, Virginia, now deceased, were married in 1958 and had three children: Laura, Rob, and Frank.

Dr. Webster has been an antique collector for more than 30 years. His major areas of interest include old tools and primitive household items. It was not until he married his second wife, Marsha, in 1997 that he became interested in the history of the Wheeling Decorating Company. To develop the desired research on this company, he and Marsha became ardent collectors of china, pottery, and glassware decorated by the Wheeling firm. This, along with close interactions with former workers and family members, has given the foundation for the information presented in his new book, *Wheeling Decorating Company*. Today, in their many travels, Jim and Marsha still seek out antique stores and malls to further add to their collection and enhance the understanding of the various aspects of this fascinating area.

Index

COLLECTOR BOOKS
informing today's collector

www.collectorbooks.com

For over two decades we have been keeping collectors informed
on trends and values in all fields of antiques and collectibles.

DOLLS, FIGURES & TEDDY BEARS

4631	**Barbie Doll** Boom, 1986–1995, Augustyniak	$18.95
2079	**Barbie Doll** Fashion, Volume I, Eames	$24.95
4846	**Barbie Doll** Fashion, Volume II, Eames	$24.95
3957	**Barbie** Exclusives, Rana	$18.95
4632	**Barbie** Exclusives, Book II, Rana	$18.95
6022	The **Barbie Doll** Years, 5th Ed., Olds	$19.95
3810	**Chatty Cathy** Dolls, Lewis	$15.95
5352	Coll. Ency. of **Barbie** Doll Exclusives & More, 2nd Ed., Augustyniak	$24.95
4863	Collector's Encyclopedia of **Vogue Dolls**, Izen/Stover	$29.95
5904	Collector's Guide to **Celebrity Dolls**, Spurgeon	$24.95
5599	Collector's Guide to **Dolls of the 1960s and 1970s**, Sabulis	$24.95
6030	Collector's Guide to **Horsman Dolls**, Jensen	$29.95
6025	**Doll Values**, Antique to Modern, 6th Ed., Moyer	$12.95
6033	**Modern Collectible Dolls**, Volume VI, Moyer	$24.95
5689	**Nippon Dolls** & Playthings, Van Patten/Lau	$29.95
5365	**Peanuts Collectibles**, Podley/Bang	$24.95
6026	**Small Dolls of the 40s & 50s**, Stover	$29.95
5253	Story of **Barbie**, 2nd Ed., Westenhouser	$24.95
5277	**Talking Toys** of the 20th Century, Lewis	$15.95
2084	**Teddy Bears, Annalee's & Steiff** Animals, 3rd Series, Mandel	$19.95
1808	Wonder of **Barbie**, Manos	$9.95
1430	World of **Barbie** Dolls, Manos	$9.95
4880	World of **Raggedy Ann** Collectibles, Avery	$24.95

TOYS & MARBLES

2333	Antique & Collectible **Marbles**, 3rd Ed., Grist	$9.95
4559	Collectible **Action Figures**, 2nd Ed., Manos	$17.95
5900	Collector's Guide to **Battery Toys**, 2nd Edition, Hultzman	$24.95
4566	Collector's Guide to **Tootsietoys**, 2nd Ed., Richter	$19.95
5169	Collector's Guide to **TV Toys** & Memorabilia, 2nd Ed., Davis/Morgan	$24.95
5593	Grist's Big Book of **Marbles**, 2nd Ed.	$24.95
3970	Grist's Machine-Made & Contemporary **Marbles**, 2nd Ed.	$9.95
5267	**Matchbox Toys**, 1947 to 1998, 3rd Ed., Johnson	$19.95
5830	**McDonald's** Collectibles, 2nd Edition, Henriques/DuVall	$24.95
5673	Modern **Candy Containers** & Novelties, Brush/Miller	$19.95
1540	Modern **Toys** 1930–1980, Baker	$19.95
5920	**Schroeder's Collectible Toys**, Antique to Modern Price Guide, 8th Ed.	$17.95
5908	**Toy Car** Collector's Guide, Johnson	$19.95

FURNITURE

3716	American **Oak** Furniture, Book II, McNerney	$12.95
1118	Antique **Oak** Furniture, Hill	$7.95
3720	Collector's Encyclopedia of **American** Furniture, Vol. III, Swedberg	$24.95
5359	Early **American** Furniture, Obbard	$12.95
3906	**Heywood-Wakefield** Modern Furniture, Rouland	$18.95
1885	**Victorian** Furniture, Our American Heritage, McNerney	$9.95
3829	**Victorian** Furniture, Our American Heritage, Book II, McNerney	$9.95

JEWELRY, HATPINS, WATCHES & PURSES

4704	Antique & Collectible **Buttons**, Wisniewski	$19.95
1748	Antique **Purses**, Revised Second Ed., Holiner	$19.95
4850	Collectible **Costume Jewelry**, Simonds	$24.95
5675	Collectible **Silver Jewelry**, Rezazadeh	$24.95
3722	Coll. Ency. of **Compacts**, Carryalls & Face Powder Boxes, Mueller	$24.95
4940	**Costume Jewelry**, A Practical Handbook & Value Guide, Rezazadeh	$24.95
5812	Fifty Years of Collectible **Fashion Jewelry**, 1925–1975, Baker	$24.95

1424	**Hatpins** & Hatpin Holders, Baker	$9.95
5695	**Ladies' Vintage Accessories**, Bruton	$24.95
1181	100 Years of Collectible **Jewelry**, 1850–1950, Baker	$9.95
4729	**Sewing Tools** & Trinkets, Thompson	$24.95
6038	**Sewing Tools** & Trinkets, Volume 2, Thompson	$24.95
6039	Signed Beauties of **Costume Jewelry**, Brown	$24.95
5620	Unsigned Beauties of **Costume Jewelry**, Brown	$24.95
4878	Vintage & Contemporary **Purse Accessories**, Gerson	$24.95
5696	Vintage & Vogue Ladies' **Compacts**, 2nd Edition, Gerson	$29.95
5923	**Vintage Jewelry** for Investment & Casual Wear, Edeen	$24.95

INDIANS, GUNS, KNIVES, TOOLS, PRIMITIVES

6021	**Arrowheads** of the Central Great Plains, Fox	$19.95
1868	Antique **Tools**, Our American Heritage, McNerney	$9.95
5616	Big Book of **Pocket Knives**, Stewart	$19.95
4943	Field Guide to Flint **Arrowheads** & Knives of the North American Indian	$9.95
3885	**Indian Artifacts** of the Midwest, Book II, Hothem	$16.95
4870	**Indian Artifacts** of the Midwest, Book III, Hothem	$18.95
5685	**Indian Artifacts** of the Midwest, Book IV, Hothem	$19.95
6132	**Modern Guns**, Identification & Values, 14th Ed., Quertermous	$14.95
2164	**Primitives**, Our American Heritage, McNerney	$9.95
1759	**Primitives**, Our American Heritage, 2nd Series, McNerney	$14.95
6031	Standard **Knife** Collector's Guide, 4th Ed., Ritchie & Stewart	$14.95
5999	**Wilderness** Survivor's Guide, Hamper	$12.95

PAPER COLLECTIBLES & BOOKS

4633	**Big Little Books**, Jacobs	$18.95
5902	**Boys' & Girls' Book** Series	$19.95
4710	Collector's Guide to **Children's Books**, 1850 to 1950, Volume I, Jones	$18.95
5153	Collector's Guide to **Children's Books**, 1850 to 1950, Volume II, Jones	$19.95
1441	Collector's Guide to **Post Cards**, Wood	$9.95
5926	**Duck Stamps**, Chappell	$9.95
2081	Guide to Collecting **Cookbooks**, Allen	$14.95
2080	Price Guide to **Cookbooks** & Recipe Leaflets, Dickinson	$9.95
3973	**Sheet Music** Reference & Price Guide, 2nd Ed., Pafik & Guiheen	$19.95
6041	Vintage **Postcards** for the Holidays, Reed	$24.95
4733	**Whitman Juvenile Books**, Brown	$17.95

GLASSWARE

5602	Anchor Hocking's **Fire-King** & More, 2nd Ed.	$24.95
5823	Collectible **Glass Shoes**, 2nd Edition, Wheatley	$24.95
5897	Coll. **Glassware** from the 40s, 50s & 60s, 6th Ed., Florence	$19.95
1810	Collector's Encyclopedia of **American Art Glass**, Shuman	$29.95
5907	Collector's Encyclopedia of **Depression Glass**, 15th Ed., Florence	$19.95
1961	Collector's Encyclopedia of **Fry Glassware**, Fry Glass Society	$24.95
1664	Collector's Encyclopedia of **Heisey Glass**, 1925–1938, Bredehoft	$24.95
3905	Collector's Encyclopedia of **Milk Glass**, Newbound	$24.95
4936	Collector's Guide to **Candy Containers**, Dezso/Poirier	$19.95
5820	Collector's Guide to **Glass Banks**, Reynolds	$24.95
4564	**Crackle Glass**, Weitman	$19.95
4941	**Crackle Glass**, Book II, Weitman	$19.95
4714	**Czechoslovakian Glass** and Collectibles, Book II, Barta/Rose	$16.95
5528	Early American **Pattern Glass**, Metz	$17.95
6125	**Elegant Glassware** of the Depression Era, 10th Ed., Florence	$24.95
3981	Evers' Standard **Cut Glass** Value Guide	$12.95
5614	Field Guide to **Pattern Glass**, McCain	$17.95
5615	Florence's **Glassware Pattern Identification** Guide, Vol. II	$19.95

4719	**Fostoria**, Etched, Carved & Cut Designs, Vol. II, Kerr	$24.95
5261	**Fostoria** Tableware, 1924 – 1943, Long/Seate	$24.95
5361	**Fostoria** Tableware, 1944 – 1986, Long/Seate	$24.95
5604	**Fostoria**, Useful & Ornamental, Long/Seate	$29.95
5899	**Glass & Ceramic Baskets**, White	$19.95
4644	**Imperial Carnival Glass**, Burns	$18.95
5827	**Kitchen Glassware** of the Depression Years, 6th Ed., Florence	$24.95
5600	Much More Early American **Pattern Glass**, Metz	$17.95
5915	**Northwood Carnival Glass**, 1908 – 1925, Burns	$19.95
6136	Pocket Guide to **Depression Glass**, 13th Ed., Florence	$12.95
6023	Standard Encyclopedia of **Carnival Glass**, 8th Ed., Edwards/Carwile	$29.95
6024	Standard **Carnival Glass** Price Guide, 13th Ed., Edwards/Carwile	$9.95
6035	Standard Encyclopedia of **Opalescent Glass**, 4th Ed., Edwards/Carwile	$24.95
4732	**Very Rare Glassware** of the Depression Years, 5th Series, Florence	$24.95

POTTERY

4927	**ABC Plates & Mugs**, Lindsay	$24.95
4929	**American Art Pottery**, Sigafoose	$24.95
4630	**American Limoges**, Limoges	$24.95
1312	**Blue & White Stoneware**, McNerney	$9.95
1959	**Blue Willow**, 2nd Ed., Gaston	$14.95
4851	Collectible **Cups & Saucers**, Harran	$18.95
1373	Collector's Encyclopedia of **American Dinnerware**, Cunningham	$24.95
4931	Collector's Encyclopedia of **Bauer Pottery**, Chipman	$24.95
5034	Collector's Encyclopedia of **California Pottery**, 2nd Ed., Chipman	$24.95
3723	Collector's Encyclopedia of **Cookie Jars**, Book II, Roerig	$24.95
4939	Collector's Encyclopedia of **Cookie Jars**, Book III, Roerig	$24.95
5748	Collector's Encyclopedia of **Fiesta**, 9th Ed., Huxford	$24.95
3961	Collector's Encyclopedia of **Early Noritake**, Alden	$24.95
3812	Collector's Encyclopedia of **Flow Blue China**, 2nd Ed., Gaston	$24.95
3431	Collector's Encyclopedia of **Homer Laughlin China**, Jasper	$24.95
1276	Collector's Encyclopedia of **Hull Pottery**, Roberts	$19.95
3962	Collector's Encyclopedia of **Lefton China**, DeLozier	$19.95
4855	Collector's Encyclopedia of **Lefton China**, Book II, DeLozier	$19.95
5609	Collector's Encyclopedia of **Limoges Porcelain**, 3rd Ed., Gaston	$29.95
2334	Collector's Encyclopedia of **Majolica Pottery**, Katz-Marks	$19.95
1358	Collector's Encyclopedia of **McCoy Pottery**, Huxford	$19.95
5677	Collector's Encyclopedia of **Niloak**, 2nd Edition, Gifford	$29.95
3837	Collector's Encyclopedia of **Nippon Porcelain**, Van Patten	$24.95
1665	Collector's Ency. of **Nippon Porcelain**, 3rd Series, Van Patten	$24.95
5053	Collector's Ency. of **Nippon Porcelain**, 5th Series, Van Patten	$24.95
5678	Collector's Ency. of **Nippon Porcelain**, 6th Series, Van Patten	$29.95
1447	Collector's Encyclopedia of **Noritake**, Van Patten	$19.95
5564	Collector's Encyclopedia of **Pickard China**, Reed	$29.95
5679	Collector's Encyclopedia of **Red Wing Art Pottery**, Dollen	$24.95
5618	Collector's Encyclopedia of **Rosemeade Pottery**, Dommel	$24.95
5841	Coll. Encyclopedia of **Roseville Pottery**, Revised, Huxford/Nickel	$24.95
5842	Coll. Encyclopedia of **Roseville Pottery**, 2nd Series, Huxford/Nickel	$24.95
5917	Collector's Encyclopedia of **Russel Wright**, 3rd Editon, Kerr	$29.95
5370	Collector's Encyclopedia of **Stangl Dinnerware**, Runge	$24.95
5921	Collector's Encyclopedia of **Stangl Artware**, Lamps, and Birds, Runge	$29.95
3314	Collector's Encyclopedia of **Van Briggle Art Pottery**, Sasicki	$24.95
5680	Collector's Guide to **Feather Edge Ware**, McAllister	$19.95
3876	Collector's Guide to **Lu-Ray Pastels**, Meehan	$18.95
3814	Collector's Guide to **Made in Japan Ceramics**, White	$18.95
4646	Collector's Guide to **Made in Japan Ceramics**, Book II, White	$18.95
1425	**Cookie Jars**, Westfall	$9.95
3440	**Cookie Jars**, Book II, Westfall	$19.95
5909	**Dresden Porcelain** Studios, Harran	$29.95
5918	Florence's Big Book of **Salt & Pepper Shakers**	$24.95

2379	**Lehner's Ency. of U.S. Marks** on Pottery, Porcelain & China	$24.95
4722	**McCoy Pottery**, Collector's Reference & Value Guide, Hanson/Nissen	$19.95
5913	**McCoy Pottery**, Volume III, Hanson & Nissen	$24.95
5691	**Post86 Fiesta**, Identification & Value Guide, Racheter	$19.95
1670	**Red Wing Collectibles**, DePasquale	$9.95
1440	**Red Wing Stoneware**, DePasquale	$9.95
6037	**Rookwood Pottery**, Nicholson & Thomas	$24.95
1632	**Salt & Pepper Shakers**, Guarnaccia	$9.95
5091	**Salt & Pepper Shakers** II, Guarnaccia	$18.95
3443	**Salt & Pepper Shakers** IV, Guarnaccia	$18.95
3738	**Shawnee Pottery**, Mangus	$24.95
4629	Turn of the Century **American Dinnerware**, 1880s–1920s, Jasper	$24.95
3327	**Watt Pottery** – Identification & Value Guide, Morris	$19.95
5924	**Zanesville Stoneware** Company, Rans, Ralston & Russell	$24.95

OTHER COLLECTIBLES

5916	Advertising **Paperweights**, Holiner & Kammerman	$24.95
5838	Advertising **Thermometers**, Merritt	$16.95
5898	Antique & Contemporary **Advertising Memorabilia**, Summers	$24.95
5814	Antique **Brass & Copper** Collectibles, Gaston	$24.95
1880	**Antique Iron**, McNerney	$9.95
3872	**Antique Tins**, Dodge	$24.95
4845	Antique **Typewriters & Office Collectibles**, Rehr	$19.95
5607	Antiquing and Collecting on the **Internet**, Parry	$12.95
1128	**Bottle** Pricing Guide, 3rd Ed., Cleveland	$7.95
3718	Collectible **Aluminum**, Grist	$16.95
5060	Collectible **Souvenir Spoons**, Bednersh	$19.95
5676	Collectible **Souvenir Spoons**, Book II, Bednersh	$29.95
5666	Collector's Encyclopedia of **Granite Ware**, Book 2, Greguire	$29.95
5836	Collector's Guide to **Antique Radios**, 5th Ed., Bunis	$19.95
3966	Collector's Guide to **Inkwells**, Identification & Values, Badders	$18.95
4947	Collector's Guide to **Inkwells**, Book II, Badders	$19.95
5681	Collector's Guide to **Lunchboxes**, White	$19.95
5621	Collector's Guide to **Online Auctions**, Hix	$12.95
4864	Collector's Guide to **Wallace Nutting Pictures**, Ivankovich	$18.95
5683	**Fishing Lure** Collectibles, Vol. 1, Murphy/Edmisten	$29.95
5911	**Flea Market Trader**, 13th Ed., Huxford	$9.95
6227	**Garage Sale & Flea Market** Annual, 11th Edition, Huxford	$19.95
4945	**G-Men and FBI Toys** and Collectibles, Whitworth	$18.95
3819	**General Store** Collectibles, Wilson	$24.95
5912	The **Heddon** Legacy, A Century of Classic **Lures**, Roberts & Pavey	$29.95
2216	**Kitchen Antiques**, 1790–1940, McNerney	$14.95
5991	**Lighting Devices** & Accessories of the 17th – 19th Centuries, Hamper	$9.95
5686	**Lighting Fixtures** of the Depression Era, Book I, Thomas	$24.95
4950	The **Lone Ranger**, Collector's Reference & Value Guide, Felbinger	$18.95
6028	Modern **Fishing Lure** Collectibles, Vol. 1, Lewis	$24.95
6131	Modern **Fishing Lure** Collectibles, Vol. 2, Lewis	$24.95
2026	**Railroad** Collectibles, 4th Ed., Baker	$14.95
5619	**Roy Rogers and Dale Evans** Toys & Memorabilia, Coyle	$24.95
6137	**Schroeder's Antiques** Price Guide, 21st Edition	$14.95
5007	**Silverplated Flatware**, Revised 4th Edition, Hagan	$18.95
6239	**Star Wars** Super Collector's Wish Book, 2nd Ed., Carlton	$29.95
6139	Summers' Guide to **Coca-Cola**, 4th Ed.	$24.95
5905	Summers' Pocket Guide to **Coca-Cola**, 3rd Ed.	$12.95
3977	Value Guide to **Gas Station Memorabilia**, Summers & Priddy	$24.95
4877	Vintage **Bar Ware**, Visakay	$24.95
5925	The Vintage Era of **Golf Club Collectibles**, John	$29.95
6010	The Vintage Era of **Golf Club Collectibles** Collector's Log, John	$9.95
6036	Vintage **Quilts**, Aug, Newman & Roy	$24.95
4935	The W.F. Cody **Buffalo Bill** Collector's Guide with Values	$24.95

This is only a partial listing of the books on antiques that are available from Collector Books. All books are well illustrated and contain current values. Most of these books are available from your local bookseller, antique dealer, or public library. If you are unable to locate certain titles in your area, you may order by mail from **COLLECTOR BOOKS**, P.O. Box 3009, Paducah, KY 42002-3009. Customers with Visa, Master Card, or Discover may phone in orders from 7:00–5:00 CT, Monday–Friday, Toll Free **1-800-626-5420**, or online at **www.collectorbooks.com**. Add $3.00 for postage for the first book ordered and 50¢ for each additional book. Include item number, title, and price when ordering. Allow 14 to 21 days for delivery.

informing today's collector

COLLECTOR BOOKS

Schroeder's ANTIQUES Price Guide

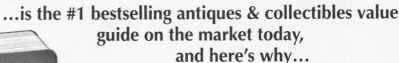

...is the #1 bestselling antiques & collectibles value guide on the market today, and here's why...

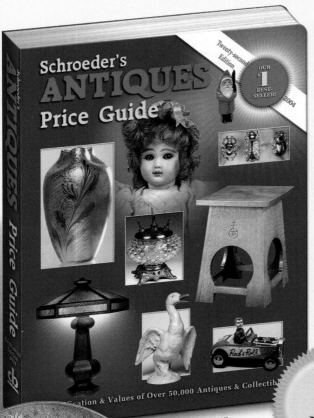

Twenty-second Edition

OUR #1 BEST-SELLER! 2004

8½" x 11"
608 pages • $14.95

Classification & Values of Over 50,000 Antiques & Collectibles

• *More than 400 advisors, well-known dealers, and top-notch collectors work together with our editors to bring you accurate information regarding pricing and identification.*

• *More than 50,000 items in over 500 categories are listed along with hundreds of sharp original photos that illustrate not only the rare and unusual, but the common, popular collectibles as well.*

• *Each large close-up shot shows important details clearly. Every subject is represented with histories and background information, a feature not found in any of our competitors' publications.*

• *Our editors keep abreast of newly developing trends, often adding several new categories a year as the need arises.*

OUR #1 BEST-SELLER!

Without doubt, you'll find
**Schroeder's Antiques
Price Guide**
the only one to buy
for reliable information and values.

If it merits the interest of today's collector, you'll find it in *Schroeder's*. And you can feel confident that the information we publish is up-to-date and accurate. Our advisors thoroughly check each category to spot inconsistencies, listings that may not be entirely reflective of market dealings, and lines too vague to be of merit. Only the best of the lot remains for publication.

COLLECTOR BOOKS
P.O. Box 3009
Paducah, KY 42002–3009
www.collectorbooks.com

cb